Orca
TIMELINE

CITIES

How Humans Live Together

MEGAN CLENDENAN

Illustrated by
SUHARU OGAWA

ORCA BOOK PUBLISHERS

Published in Canada and the United States in 2023 by Orca Book Publishers.
orcabook.com

Library and Archives Canada Cataloguing in Publication
Title: Cities : how humans live together / Megan Clendenan ; illustrated by Suharu Ogawa.
Names: Clendenan, Megan, 1977- author. | Ogawa, Suharu, 1979- illustrator.
Description: Series statement: Orca timeline ; 3 | Includes bibliographical references and index.
Identifiers: Canadiana (print) 20220277214 | Canadiana (ebook) 20220277222 |
ISBN 9781459831469 (hardcover) | ISBN 9781459831476 (PDF) | ISBN 9781459831483 (EPUB)
Subjects: LCSH: City and town life—Juvenile literature. | LCSH: Cities and towns—Juvenile literature. |
LCSH: City dwellers—Juvenile literature. | LCSH: Urban ecology (Sociology)—Juvenile literature.
Classification: LCC HT152 .C54 2023 | DDC j307.76—dc23

Library of Congress Control Number: 2022941566

Summary: Part of the nonfiction Orca Timeline series for middle-grade readers, this illustrated book examines the past, present and future of cities around the world.

Orca Book Publishers is committed to reducing the consumption of nonrenewable resources in the production of our books. We make every effort to use materials that support a sustainable future.

Orca Book Publishers gratefully acknowledges the support for its publishing programs provided by the following agencies: the Government of Canada, the Canada Council for the Arts and the Province of British Columbia through the BC Arts Council and the Book Publishing Tax Credit.

Cover and interior artwork by Suharu Ogawa
Design by Dahlia Yuen
Edited by Kirstie Hudson
Author photo by Dave Clendenan
Illustrator photo by Darcy MacQuarrie

Printed and bound in South Korea.

26 25 24 23 • 1 2 3 4

*For all my lovely neighbors, for transforming
our city street into a community.*

Like living in a rainbow! Located in Kyiv, Ukraine, this colorful neighborhood called Comfort Town has green courtyards away from cars as well as playing fields, schools and shops.

MENSENT PHOTOGRAPHY/GETTY IMAGES

Contents

Introduction

Have you ever wondered what it was like to live in a city 100 years ago? How about 1,000? What about 50 years in the future? I once lived in London, England, a city that is almost 2,000 years old. It has narrow cobblestone streets, markets that have sold food for hundreds of years and glass skyscrapers that tower high above the city. As I wandered the streets, I wondered, Were the streets once shared with horses or goats? Was the water safe to drink? Where did people put their garbage? Could you go play at a park with your friends? Did people feel safe walking around? If you had to go to the bathroom, was there one available?

In other words, what does a city need to become a good place to live for everyone?

1

Researchers have found that there are qualities in a city that make people feel happy living there. They include feeling safe, being able to travel about easily for their daily activities, having green space nearby so they can enjoy nature, and being part of a community. People also need to feel welcome. And they need clean air to breathe, safe water to drink and healthy food readily available.

For the last 9,000 years, we humans have been putting our heads together to build our cities to suit our needs—but there have been ups and downs along the way. Today's cities deal with many of the same issues as cities of the past, as well as new ones. Cities produce at least 60 percent of global greenhouse gas *emissions*, and they face big challenges from the effects of the *climate crisis*, like hurricanes and heat waves.

The ancient city of Shibam, Yemen, was designed so that everyone could easily walk to their daily activities. Can cities today create more compact neighborhoods that mean less travel and more time to play? In the ancient Aztec city of Tenochtitlán, in today's Mexico, residents grew crops using waste products from the city. Is *zero waste* possible for today's cities? We'll explore how cities have changed through time and how we can best design city life for the future using ideas from the past.

When better services or sustainable ideas are put into place in cities—such as solar panels, rooftop farms or more buses and bike lanes—it can make life better for a huge number of people. That's good news, because by 2050 an estimated 70 percent of the world's population will live in cities. Let's go discover what might make a more sustainable and welcoming city for today and tomorrow.

People relax by Cheonggyecheon Stream in Seoul. Hidden under concrete for many years, the stream was restored in 2005. These days, on average, it attracts 64,000 visitors daily.
RICHARD SHARROCKS/
GETTY IMAGES

Ur, Mesopotamia
2000 BCE

Rome
200

Beijing
1300

Brasília, Brazil
1956–1960

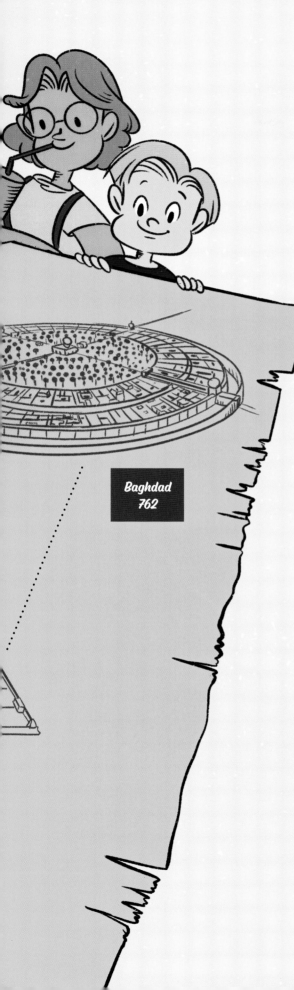

Baghdad
762

One

Mapping It Out

Only 9,000 years ago (give or take!), cities didn't exist. Today about four billion people—about half the world's population—live in cities. This number could rise to seven billion by 2050! What is a city? It turns out there's not just one definition that everyone agrees on. Some countries define cities based on the number of residents, others by the type of work done by the people living there. City populations range from 1,500 to 50,000 to millions of people. But what makes a city a good place for people to live? Is it its shape or size? The number of services it has, like libraries, hospitals or shops? Is it having parks where you can enjoy nature and see your friends? Or is it having a low level of crime, pollution and noise? Cities have changed a lot over time. Let's take a look at how they got started and what they might look like in the future.

LOCATION, LOCATION, LOCATION

Permanent settlements began to take root when people discovered they could stay in one place and grow grains such as barley and emmer (an ancient kind of wheat) instead of moving around to find food the way their ancestors had. The first cities showed up around 7500 BCE in Mesopotamia, 3300 BCE in the Indus Valley of present-day Pakistan and India, and 3100 BCE in Egypt. If you had a lake or river for water, plus some invader-stopping geography such as an island or a hilltop with good views of approaching enemies, you had yourself a good location for a city. If you were a ruler, you'd likely build a temple or palace right in the center of your city.

Babylon, in ancient Mesopotamia, was surrounded by walls that were 30 to 40 feet (9 to 12 meters) high and wide enough to accommodate chariot races.

Let's Trade

With grain safely stored behind temple walls and farmers harvesting more food than they could eat, some people were freed up to do other jobs, like weave cloth or make baskets. A farmer could now trade grain for a pottery jar at the local market. Merchants traded goods with nearby cities, and towns were established along trade routes such as the **Silk Road**.

One of the World's First Megacities

Around 2,000 years ago, one million people lived in ancient Rome. After developing their own type of concrete in the first century, Romans built monuments that still stand today. The Colosseum was an amphitheater that hosted gladiator battles and wild-animal hunts. Wealthy Romans lived well, but most people lived in crowded buildings called insulae, which were apartment buildings so poorly built that they sometimes collapsed. Rome faced constant threats. In 410 CE invaders held the city hostage for three days until they were given 2 tons (1.8 metric tons) of gold, 13 tons (11.8 metric tons) of silver, 4,000 silk tunics, 3,000 fleeces and 3,000 pounds (1,361 kilograms) of black pepper.

Population of Megacities Through Time

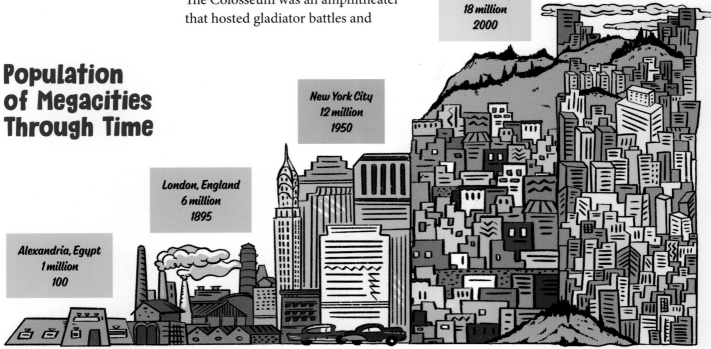

Dhaka, Bangladesh
21 million
2020

Mexico City
18 million
2000

New York City
12 million
1950

London, England
6 million
1895

Alexandria, Egypt
1 million
100

If You Lived in... Ur, Mesopotamia

Around 2000 BCE, Ur was a busy city of 65,000 people next to the Euphrates River, in today's Iraq. Many people farmed, but your parents might also have woven cloth or made pottery. You lived in a mud-brick house with a central courtyard, on a narrow, winding street that provided shade from the fierce Mesopotamian sun. After practicing letter-writing on clay, you played board games carved on bricks or raced clay model boats.

Petra, Jordan, a busy trade city between 400 BCE and 100 BCE, nestles into sandstone mountains that provided a natural defense. There was high ground in case of attack, and water springs for residents.

CITIES SHAPE UP

If you walk around your city or town, you might notice that some streets are wide and others are narrow. Some run in straight lines, others curve. Some cities simply grew outward as new arrivals set up homes on the outskirts. In other places they stuck to a plan. Shapes, symmetry and patterns—if you think that sounds like geometry, you're right. Geometry has guided *city planners* in all directions, so sharpen your pencil and grab your ruler.

Grid

In a grid system, the streets are laid out in evenly spaced horizontal and perpendicular lines. They are often numbered, making it easy to figure out where you are and how to get where you want to go. In Alexandria, Egypt, city planners marked lines for future roads with barley flour. But legend has it they had to work quickly before the seagulls ate the markings.

Fractal

In the 1000s, Benin City, known then as Edo, was the capital of an African empire in today's Nigeria. Edo was built in a mathematical pattern of symmetry and repetition now known as *fractal* design.

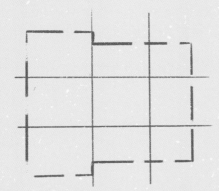

Square

In the 1300s, Beijing was built with a series of squares inspired by *feng shui*. Straight roads divided the city into nine equal sectors with nine north-to-south avenues that were nine chariot tracks wide.

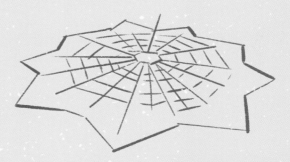

Star-Shaped

The star-shaped design of Palmanova, Italy, helped it fend off invasions and cannon fire by leaving no blind spots where attackers could evade detection.

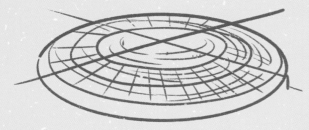

Circle

In 762, Baghdad was shaped like a circle. More than 100,000 carpenters, architects, engineers, blacksmiths and laborers used kiln-fired bricks glued together with reeds to build the circular wall. There were 1,000 mosques, 65,000 public baths, palaces, a racetrack and a paper factory.

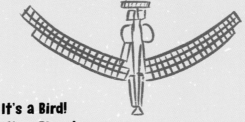

It's a Bird!
It's a Plane!

Brasilia, the capital of Brazil, was built in just 41 months (1956–1960) from an architect's sketch. From the air it resembles an airplane, a bird or a dragonfly. The central city has symmetrical streets lined with government buildings and tall apartments. Built for 500,000 residents, today more than 4.8 million people live in the surrounding *suburbs* and settlements.

GROW AND DIVIDE

Whatever shape cities took, by the 1800s many were growing quickly. The **Industrial Revolution** meant new factories, and people seeking jobs moved away from rural areas. But many people discovered the city wasn't the greatest place to live. While wealthy people lived in large homes, most of the factory workers lived in overcrowded and unsafe buildings that stank of **coal** smoke and **sewage**. Clean water and toilets were not easy to find, and many people got sick from diseases such as **typhoid** and **cholera**. By the mid-1800s, engineers and city planners had new ideas for how to improve life in cities, but they weren't always good for everyone.

Widening the Streets

In 1853, in Paris, ruler Napoleon III desired a fashionable, modern Paris that would show off his military might. He commanded a city official named Georges-Eugène Haussmann to reshape Paris. Haussmann flattened the narrow maze of streets that held the crowded tenement buildings where many people lived. Twelve thousand buildings were demolished. They were replaced with wide boulevards that military troops could easily march down, as well as city parks, hospitals, a new opera building and apartments for wealthy people. The city's redesign forced 350,000 people from their homes, and the displaced people moved to the outskirts of Paris. This division of rich and poor remains in Paris today.

Barcelona's New Grid

In the mid-1850s Barcelona was an industrial city of 187,000 people, bursting at the seams of its medieval walls. There was no space left for new homes, so some were built on arches in the middle of streets. An engineer named Ildefons Cerdà suggested a street grid that would join the old city with nearby villages to create a larger metropolis. He used scientific observations to figure out what people needed in a city, such as markets, hospitals and schools. He even calculated how much air each citizen would need to breathe.

City Zones

In 1898 in England, Ebenezer Howard came up with the idea of a "garden city" to address the problem of crowded and unsafe conditions in industrial cities. It would be divided into zones for living and working, to keep polluting factories away from homes. While the concept of a garden city never took off, since then many cities have used *zoning bylaws* to separate different functions. While zoning has benefits, it also has downsides. Where you live might be far from where your parents work. Sometimes zoning increases inequality. For example, some cities have bylaws that allow only large homes to be built in certain areas. Apartment buildings and smaller homes aren't allowed there. Those same areas are often the ones with the best schools and the most parks.

A city built with geometry! Barcelona's Eixample neighborhood features a grid pattern with straight lines, angles, octagons and squares.
POL ALBARRÁN/GETTY IMAGES

When You Gotta Go: A Social Event

In ancient Rome, going to the bathroom in public meant sharing the space with as many as 20 other men. Only men used these public toilets—women had to hold it until they got home. A channel of water ran across the floor in front of each row of seats, and moss or a sea sponge on a stick served as toilet paper.

Like many cities around the world, Mumbai has both tall towers and tiny houses and is home to both millionaires and people living with very little.
ANDREY ARMYAGOV/SHUTTERSTOCK.COM

In the 1980s, Orangi Town, an edge city of Karachi, Pakistan, had a population of more than one million people but no sewers. Residents wanted to clean up their streets, so they built their own *sewer system*.

A City Next to the City

Like 1800s London, England, today's cities are growing so rapidly that it's challenging to provide enough water, electricity and housing for new arrivals. At the edge of large cities such as Nairobi and Rio de Janeiro, huge settlements are built by people who arrive from rural places, seeking work and other opportunities. More than one billion people worldwide live in these types of settlements, and the number goes up every year. Once called slums, barrios, favelas or shantytowns, they are known outside of North America as "edge" or "arrival" cities.

Mumbai is filled with skyscrapers, mansions and Bollywood film studios. Next door is the edge city of Dharavi, India, where an estimated one million people live in an area of 0.8 square miles (2.1 square kilometers). Although access to toilets, electricity and running water is challenging, and many live in poverty, people in Dharavi have found ways to build community. Many people run small businesses, and there are health clinics, grocery stores, restaurants and salons. Businesses in Dharavi contribute more than $1 billion to Mumbai's economy.

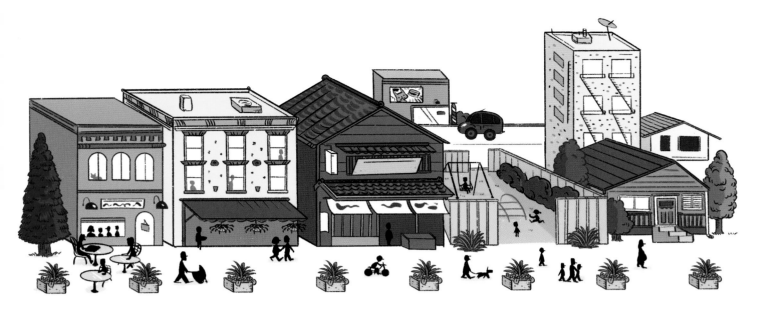

CITIES UNDER CONSTRUCTION

Creating cities for today and tomorrow that are healthy and enjoyable for everyone means solving some big problems. How do you build enough housing, and what should it look like? Where should hospitals, schools and shops go? Water and public bathrooms? How about a nice park to visit? And what about making sure everyone feels welcome? There's a lot to think about.

A Goldilocks Neighborhood?

What makes people happy in a city? Researchers have found that when people in cities feel safe, know their neighbors, have nearby green spaces and can easily connect with friends, they feel happier. There seems to be a Goldilocks type of neighborhood that makes people happy—not too big and not too small! One way to create this is to build communities that have a mix of houses, duplexes and apartments, and also restaurants, grocery stores, schools, parks and businesses. If you can live, work and go to school in your neighborhood, it means less traveling and more time for play. Just right!

Using Old Spaces

Abandoned industrial buildings, closed railways or factories can be repurposed as new recreation spaces or neighborhoods. In Melbourne, Australia, a stretch of industrial docks along the Yarra River sat unused for decades. Today it's filled with apartments, parks, a stadium, restaurants and a long boardwalk where people can enjoy the water views.

But there are times when attempts to improve a city have negative consequences, such as in Los Angeles in the 1950s, when a thriving Mexican American community was displaced to build Dodger Stadium. Sometimes an area suddenly becomes popular, and new restaurants and shops open. But what happens to the people and shops who are already there? *Gentrification* is the term for what happens when a neighborhood, usually poorer, changes as wealthier people move in and create new housing, restaurants or shops. Rents tend to increase, and many current residents are forced to leave because they can no longer afford to live there.

People gather in the Square Louise Michel in Montmartre, Paris, to visit with friends, watch buskers and enjoy a view of the city.
PIERRE OGERON/GETTY IMAGES

SPACES AND PLACES FOR EVERYONE

Public space gives people in cities a place to come together, meet their friends and neighbors and feel like they are part of a community. It includes such areas as plazas, parks and streets—for example, the Champs-Élysées in Paris or Central Park in New York. Sometimes areas are designed around a central monument or a civic building. Some allow thousands of people to participate in cultural activities. Others are small neighborhood spaces where social connections are made daily, like greeting neighbors at your local park or chatting to friends on the sidewalk in front of your apartment.

Let's Talk

In the 400s, the city of Athens hummed with energy and conversation. Gymnasiums, theaters, stadiums, markets and festivals brought people together. Athens was where **democracy** began, and a public square, called the Agora, was where people came to debate and vote (you could only vote if you were male and not a slave!). The Roman Forum was a similar place, the center of city life in ancient Rome, with theater, sports and lively markets.

A Place to Play

Playing ball or sitting under a tree with friends is not only fun, it's good for your health! But until well into the 1800s, most cities had no parks. And the few parks that did exist weren't always open to everyone. In cities today and in the past, people with more money or power have easier access to resources like parks, libraries and schools than do people from lower-income communities and communities of color. In Chicago, more than half of the $500 million spent on parks between 2011 and 2014 went to 10 mostly wealthy areas of the city's 77 neighborhoods. A group of volunteers pushed for change, and today 99 percent of low-income residents live within 10 minutes of a park.

Beach Break in the City

In the heat of summer, it's nice to hit the beach, even in the middle of Paris. Each summer the city closes part of an expressway and creates the Paris Plages event, a seaside adventure with swimming, sand, beach chairs, play equipment, ice-cream stands, board games and lots of fun activities and music. The event is hugely popular with Parisians and tourists alike.

Sidewalk and Street Games

In all cities over time, children have invented or adapted games to play wherever they find space, whether that's the sidewalk, a back alley or a quiet street. These games are played today in cities worldwide:

> hopscotch, leapfrog and tag
> marble, pebble or bottle-cap tossing
> soccer, catch or street hockey

Where concrete flood walls used to be, this mangrove forest in central Sanya City, China, now helps soak up tropical storms to reduce flooding as well as create a healthy marine environment.
SANAYA MANGROVE PARK, TURENSCAPE

WORKING WITH THE WEATHER

Cities have always had to fend off invaders, but today there's a new challenge—the climate crisis. With rising global temperatures and changing weather patterns, leaders need to figure out how best to protect their citizens against floods, heat waves, rising seas and forest fires.

Slowing Superstorms

Billions of oysters were once found in the Hudson River estuary in New York City, growing in reefs as high as 20 feet (6 meters) that reduced the damaging effects of storms by breaking up large waves. But pollution and industrial activities in the harbor destroyed the oysters, leaving the city unprotected.

When Superstorm Sandy hit New York City on October 29, 2012, it flooded buildings, streets and subway tunnels, destroyed homes, knocked out power for millions of people and forced patients to evacuate hospitals. Afterward city leaders, planners and engineers got to work planning for the next storm. Installing floodgates and building huge seawalls across the harbor were some of their ideas. But another idea is taking shape: building walls made out of dried oyster shells that are "seeded" with living oyster larvae. This will help to create new reefs that will one day help protect the city like the original oyster reefs used to.

Sponge City

To take on storms and reduce the chance of flooding, cities need to act like sponges. Shanghai is slowly replacing concrete embankments with **wetlands**, adding green rooftops to buildings and planting **rain gardens** to soak up water instead of allowing it to flood the city. All this greenery has another excellent benefit— it has a cooling effect. Cities contain huge areas of concrete and asphalt, so they heat up quickly and stay hotter longer than the surrounding countryside—they become **urban heat islands**. Shade from trees can lower the temperature, but you still might want to jump in a pool to cool down!

Bridges high in the sky:

How about skyscrapers linked by bridges? Skybridges connect buildings on a level above the street, offering new public spaces that include gardens, play spaces and trees.

Going green:

Natural infrastructure can help cities weather the climate crisis. Wetlands, mangrove forests and oyster reefs absorb wave energy while also filtering pollutants from the water and air, and give people access to green spaces.

Smart cities:

How about sensors that help people predict traffic or air quality? They could also be used to track energy use or see how full garbage cans are. Today's cities are already starting to use sensors to provide real-time information that will improve quality of life.

Shibam, Yemen
1500s

Paris
1828

Chicago
1920s

Two
Getting Around the City

Brooklyn 1894

San Francisco, 2018

Living in a city means going places! To school or work, to meet friends, to buy food or to go to the doctor. Researchers have found that the less time people have to spend traveling, and the easier and safer it is to get places, the happier they are. People like to catch a clean bus, enter a well-lit subway station or use a sidewalk separated from speeding cars. But in most cities today, cars are polluting the air and taking up huge amounts of space. How can cities make transportation more accessible to everyone? Let's find out whether the cities of the past can help us design the transportation we need and want in the future.

Hong Kong is one of the world's most walkable cities. Eighty-five percent of residents live within walking distance of a car-free public space such as a park or square.
DIDIER MARTI/GETTY IMAGES

WALKING ONLY

In ancient cities most people walked everywhere. Ancient Rome packed a million people into an area not much bigger than 2 miles (3.2 kilometers) in diameter. The narrow streets were crowded. For several centuries wagons and carriages weren't allowed during the first 10 hours of the day unless they were bringing in fresh fruit and vegetables or were carrying priests or royalty. Everyone else had to walk.

One Step at a Time

Research has shown that if cities create safe, pleasant spaces for walking, more people tie up their shoes and start strolling. To make today's cities more walkable, there must be paths that feel safe, separate from cars and noise; things to see or do, such as shops; and shade and benches to rest on along the way. A number of cities have created pedestrian-focused spaces, including Copenhagen and San Francisco. The city of Helsinki plans to connect neighborhoods with safe walking paths. That will mean less pollution from cars and more exercise for people—a win-win!

If You Lived in...Shibam, Yemen

In Shibam in the 1500s, towers constructed of sun-dried mud bricks rose as high as eight stories. Livestock, grain and tools were stored on the ground floors, elderly people lived on the lower floors, and families with children occupied the upper floors. You might have been one of the first people in history to live in a tall building. The buildings cast welcome shade on the streets below, so people could stop for a conversation and kids could play a game in the street. Walking across the city didn't take long, and some buildings were connected by bridges, allowing you to pop over to visit a neighbor in the next building without even going down to the street.

Shibam's mud-brick architecture is perfect for the hot desert climate—the bricks absorb heat from the sun during the day, then slowly release it at night.
CHRISTOPHE BOISVIEUX/GETTY IMAGES

PEDAL POWER

In the 1880s the *safety bicycle* was invented, and cycling soon became a popular way to whiz to work or school faster than on foot. Riding a bicycle with the wind in your hair (no helmets back then!) felt like freedom. In 1894 Brooklyn opened one of the nation's first bicycle paths. Ten thousand cyclists used it the first day. Bicycling is also good for the planet. The average North American passenger car produces 12.5 ounces of carbon dioxide per mile (219 grams per kilometer), so switching from a car to a bicycle for even some trips each week will eliminate a lot of emissions.

Kingdom of Bicycles

In China the bicycle was once the best way to get around cities. Cars were unaffordable for most people, and trips in the city were short enough to bike easily. The morning **commute** was a sea of bicycles. In 1988 in Beijing, 76 percent of the road space was taken up by bicycles. A bicycle known as the Flying Pigeon was the most popular. From 1981 to 1988, the number of bikes in China increased from 77 million to 225 million. Today, even though car traffic snarls up cities across the country, more than 60 percent of all urban trips are still made on foot or by bicycle (many of the bikes are electric).

All-Weather Vehicle

People in Copenhagen love to bike—and they prove it by biking not just on sunny days but through rain, hail and even snow! Sixty-two percent of all trips to work and school in Copenhagen are done by bicycle. Collectively, commuters, couriers and families travel 894,775 miles (1.44 million kilometers) each day on 250 miles (400 kilometers) of bicycle-only paths, on bikes of all kinds, from ones with wicker baskets to cargo bikes full of kids and groceries. Bike lanes in Copenhagen can be as crowded as car traffic in other cities.

With so many bikes traveling around Copenhagen, there need to be places to park them.
OLESYA KUZNETSOVA/
SHUTTERSTOCK.COM

In 1917 there were about 50,000 bicycle police in the United States. Bicycles were the fastest thing on the road at that time and the best way for officers to chase thieves.

NEXT STOP, PLEASE!

As cities have grown, so has the time it takes to travel across them. In 1828 the omnibus, a large horse-drawn wagon designed to hold 12 to 14 people, clattered through the streets of Paris. It was a bumpy, cushion-free journey over rough roads, but people still jumped on board to catch a ride. The omnibus was one of the first kinds of urban public transportation. Today, in cities around the world, millions of people gather at bus stops or head down steep escalators to underground subway stations. In Tokyo, the subway is the fastest, easiest and most affordable way to whisk from one end of the city to the other.

Watch Your Step

The first urban railway was a horsecar system, with teams of horses pulling trams along tracks. In 1860 New York City's horsecar fleet transported 36 million passengers that year alone. But the system had challenges. The horses could only work for about two to four hours before tiring, so as many as 10 horses were needed to operate each car. Horses also produced mountains of manure and quite the stench! In New York City in 1881, 2,700 street sweepers cleaned up 2.5 million tons of horse poop.

Streetcars Start Up

By 1900 most cities in North America had replaced horsecar railways with electric streetcars, sometimes called trolley cars, which were powered by overhead electric cables. Streetcar lines stretched cities even farther outward than horsecars had. By 1917 there were 45,000 miles (72,000 kilometers) of streetcar tracks in the United States, carrying millions of riders where they wanted to go.

Hong Kong
2022

San Francisco
1947

Citizens and streetcars pack the streets of Chicago in the 1920s. In 1914 a ticket to ride a streetcar cost 5 cents, which is about $1.10 in today's money.
ROBERT N. DENNIS COLLECTION OF STEREOSCOPIC VIEWS/WIKIMEDIA COMMONS/PUBLIC DOMAIN

 If You Lived in...Chicago, Illinois

In 1920s Chicago, you rarely had to wait more than a few minutes for a streetcar. Pedestrians, farmers' wagons, cyclists and streetcars shared the street with the occasional car or truck. You'd enter the streetcar by the rear door, have your fare taken by the conductor, who'd signal the driver with a bell once everyone was aboard, and off you'd go. You might travel to the beaches of Lake Michigan, to downtown museums or to the amusement park to ride a roller coaster. Streetcars also transported prisoners and hospital patients, carried mail and plowed snow. There were even special "funeral cars" that took funeral parties, including the casket, to the cemetery.

SOME TRAINS TRAVEL OVERGROUND...

Steam trains blasted into cities in England in the 1830s, starting with Manchester, moving passengers 10 miles (16 kilometers) or more in 30 minutes. People could now live far from where they worked and commute into the city by train. In 1801 London was 5 miles (8 kilometers) from east to west. By 1901 the city measured more than 17 miles (27 kilometers) across, with suburbs built up around railway stations outside the city center.

Some Travel Underground...

In the late 1850s London's streets were so filled with carts, horses, wagons and people that city officials decided to build a new railway—underground. Tunnels were dug under existing roads, and on January 10, 1863, more than 30,000 people took gas-lit wooden carriages pulled by steam trains from Paddington to Farringdon. It was the world's first subway. By 1900 commuters were riding subways in Paris, Boston, Budapest, Glasgow and Chicago, and today more than 160 cities worldwide have underground subways.

Some Hover!

The Shanghai Maglev train has no wheels! Instead it uses electromagnetic levitation to hover above the tracks and move without ever touching them. Powerful electromagnets lift the entire train about 0.4 inches (10 millimeters) above the track, which is called a guideway. More electromagnets propel the train forward at a cruising speed of 268 miles per hour (431 kilometers per hour). Visitors who arrive at Shanghai Pudong International Airport can hop on the Maglev and travel 19 miles (30 kilometers) to the eastern side of the city in under eight minutes.

Even faster? China has launched an even swifter Maglev train with a top speed of 373 miles per hour (600 kilometers per hour).
CYO BO/SHUTTERSTOCK.COM

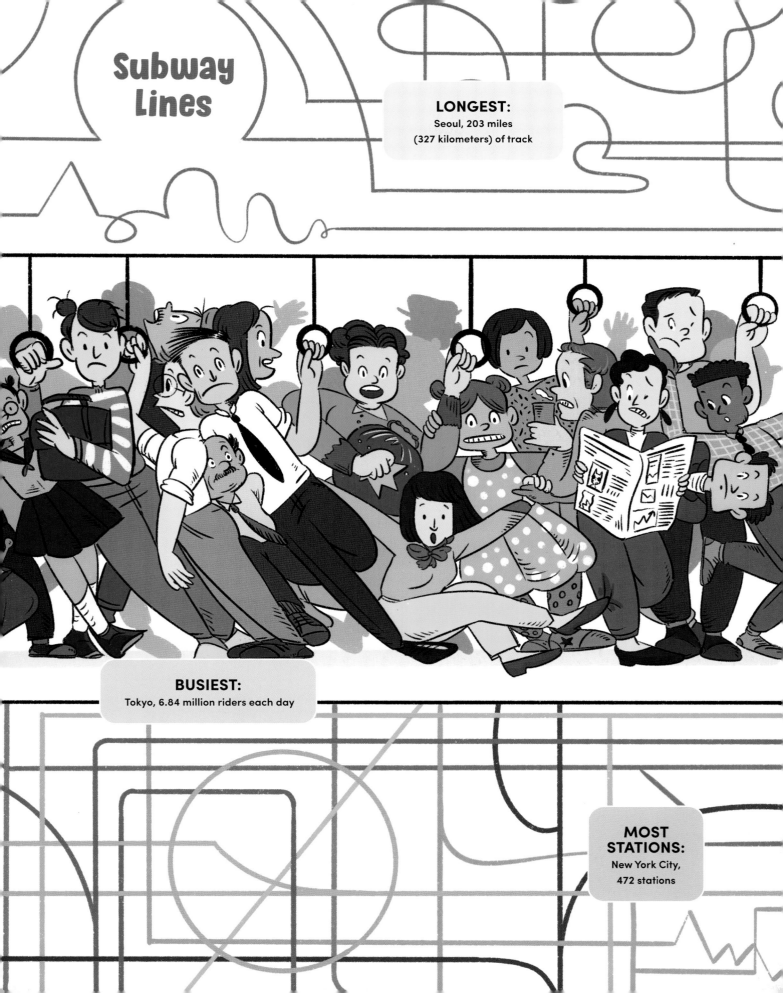

Subway Lines

LONGEST:
Seoul, 203 miles
(327 kilometers) of track

BUSIEST:
Tokyo, 6.84 million riders each day

MOST STATIONS:
New York City,
472 stations

WANT A RIDE?

Besides buses, bikes and trains, there are other ways to get around. In Lisbon, funiculars help both locals and tourists ascend the city's many hills. In Bangkok, three-wheeled motorized tuk-tuks zoom through the streets. Cities around the world have created unique types of public transit that help people get across town.

Three-Wheeled Human-Powered Taxi

In Dhaka, Bangladesh, there are hundreds of thousands of cycle rickshaws. They don't burn *fossil fuels*, fares are affordable for most people, and they can navigate narrow roads that other vehicles cannot. But driving them is not an easy job, and they are at times blamed for traffic jams. While cycle rickshaws have been banned in places, they remain popular, both as a way to earn a living and as a low-cost, easy way to get around the city.

Mapping Minibuses

In some African cities, including Nairobi (Kenya), Addis Ababa (Ethiopia) and Accra (Ghana), small privately owned buses transport millions of people across town every day. Often called informal buses, they offer flexible stops and schedules, have affordable fares and cover areas not served by regular buses. While popular, they can be challenging, as people often have to guess the schedule. To help users navigate minibus systems, people have created digital maps for mobile phones to help people find when and where they can catch a ride.

Ride the Skies

Imagine peacefully soaring over the city, floating over office buildings, sports fields and homes, with a view of the snow-capped Andes mountains. Sounds like you'd need an airplane, right? Not in La Paz, Bolivia, where more than 230,000 people each day board a cable car for a ride in the sky to work or school. Cable cars arrive every 12 seconds at 26 stations on a 6.2-mile (10-kilometer) route. It's the highest and longest urban cable-car system in the world. Before this system, there was only a busy, congested highway, and people spent hours getting to and from work.

Want a bird's-eye view of a city? Catch a ride on a cable car in La Paz, Bolivia.
SAIKO3P/GETTY IMAGES

HEY, SLOW DOWN!

City streets through time have always been shared. People walked or rode horses. Market stalls sold food. Children played. When new forms of transportation arrived, there was often conflict. When horsecar railways were introduced, some people thought the metal tracks were dangerous and would turn carriages over. Horses would at times bolt in panic when nearing a fast-moving cyclist. Pedestrians and cyclists jostled for space, collisions occurred, and fistfights took place. When cars appeared, it was no different. They moved fast, took up too much space and collided with pedestrians and other cars. People tried to ban cars and keep speed limits low, but it didn't work. Streets became more for cars and less for other users.

There are a billion parking spots in the United States, four for every car in the country.

Fast Cars

In the 1950s the US government gave money to cities to build roads out to new suburbs. Engineers designed *freeways*, which allowed motor vehicles to travel at high speeds through and around the city. Cities began to spread outward, changing how many people lived. New developments with huge parking lots—stores, schools, churches and community centers—were often located near the new freeways, far from people's homes.

Without a car, it became more difficult for people to get around. Sprawling cities have other consequences. Houston grew by 63 percent between 1997 and 2017. This means that 1,000 square kilometers of land—an area equivalent to almost 187,000 football fields—were covered in impervious surfaces such as concrete. These surfaces don't absorb water, increasing flood risk and making events such as Hurricane Harvey in 2017 worse.

Fighting Back

Freeways are convenient if you own a car, but their construction has often destroyed communities. In North America, low-income neighborhoods and communities of color are usually affected the most. Although people fight against the freeways, it is a difficult battle to win.

In some cases, though, freeway projects have been stopped. In the 1960s writer and activist Jane Jacobs helped prevent the construction of a freeway through Manhattan in New York City and an expressway in her Toronto neighborhood. She asked a lot of questions about why and how cities are planned, and introduced new ideas that focused more on communities and less on cars. Even so, space for cars, such as roads and parking lots, now takes up as much as 50 percent of all land in a North American city. At the same time, sidewalks have both shrunk in size or don't exist at all. So who is the city for anyway?

Around 1970 in Vancouver, BC, a once thriving Black community known as Hogan's Alley was displaced to construct a freeway.

CANADA

HOGAN'S ALLEY

63

CITIES OPEN TO ALL

Everyone who lives in a city wants and needs to get to school or work, meet their friends and buy food for dinner. Public transportation is a low-cost way to get around compared to owning a car. It also reduces traffic and air pollution. But public transportation doesn't always keep up with a rising population, and it doesn't always reach people in all parts of a city. When it's not available, it means that some people—often seniors, young people, individuals with disabilities or people with lower incomes—aren't able to move around their city. But it doesn't have to be that way.

Build It and They Will Ride

In Bogotá, Colombia, in the 1990s, roads were choked with cars and pollution. Only about 19 percent of the population could afford a car—everyone else struggled to get around. In 1999 Enrique Peñalosa, Bogotá's mayor, decided to create a new bus network through the city. By 2012 the city had 12 rapid bus lines and 1,500 buses that transported around 1.5 million passengers each day. Air pollution was reduced by about 40 percent.

Rolling on Through

For the hundreds of millions of people with disabilities, such as wheelchair users or those with vision or hearing loss, getting around can be full of obstacles, even with a public transit system. In the 1970s in Berkeley, California, disability activists made concrete ramps at corners where people in wheelchairs needed to travel but couldn't due to high, sharp curbs. Today curbs that slope down to the road are found in many cities, and many are designed with raised bumps that help alert visually impaired people using a cane that there is a change in the slope of the pavement.

Small signs can have a big effect. The raised dots of braille help visually impaired people use the public transit system with greater ease and confidence.
TAEWAFEEL/SHUTTERSTOCK.COM

Accessible Alerts

Technology is another way to help cities improve accessibility. Some cities have digital maps with specific information to help wheelchair users. For example, they can show how steep a street is or whether there are stairs without a ramp. Other digital apps use audio cues to help visually impaired travelers navigate the city. And in Vancouver, British Columbia, 8,400 bus stops now include **braille** information that visually impaired people can touch and read.

In Curitiba, Brazil, comfortable, affordable, fast buses run frequently, and around 70 to 80 percent of Curitiba's commuters use the buses to travel to work. One study showed the system had replaced 27 million car journeys per year and significantly reduced air pollution.

A LANE FOR EVERYONE

As we've seen, early cities were more compact, allowing people to walk to daily activities, and when public transportation was introduced, people jumped on board. We've now come full circle. More cities are working to create safe paths through the city for walking and biking. In the Netherlands, kids as young as four are pumping their legs on a bicycle school bus. Each bike bus is designed for an adult driver and 11 kids up to the age of 12. When streets are designed with lanes for cars, lanes for buses, lanes for bicycles and wide sidewalks for people, everyone wins. It means less pollution, less traffic and more active people!

Slower Streets

In 2001, in the Dutch city of Drachten, a **traffic engineer** named Hans Monderman created a four-way intersection with no traffic lights or signs in hopes of cutting down on accidents. Because no one had the right-of-way, everyone paid more attention. Pedestrians looked carefully before crossing the street. Drivers slowed down. Cyclists used hand signals. To demonstrate it was safe, Monderman walked backward through the intersection with his eyes closed. After it had been in place for a year, results showed that there were half as many accidents, but more traffic overall. While this wouldn't work for every intersection, it might work in some places.

**If You Lived in...
Groningen,
Netherlands**

If you lived in Groningen today, you would probably have more bicycles than people in your household. You might live on a narrow lane lined with houses or small apartments. You might play tag or hopscotch or toss a ball with friends on the street. When cars drive by, they go as slow as snails and give you time to move your game to the side. All space is shared. People, not cars, come first on this **living street**, or woonerf, a space for all users, rather than just for cars to travel from A to B.

Sharing Is Caring

Many cities, including Berlin, Paris, Amsterdam, London, Seoul, Rio de Janeiro and Mexico City, have bike-sharing programs. Bikes are placed in busy parts of the city, and for a small fee you can borrow the bike for the hour or the day and then return it to another bike station. Shared bikes, taxis, scooters…the more shared resources a city has, the more options there are to get around.

The 15-Minute City

What if you could walk or bike everywhere you needed to go in 15 minutes—to school, work, the grocery store, a community center, the library or a hospital? That's the idea behind the "15-minute city," a concept that city planners in Paris, Melbourne, Chengdu (China) and other cities hope to turn into a reality.

The Future of City Transit Is Now

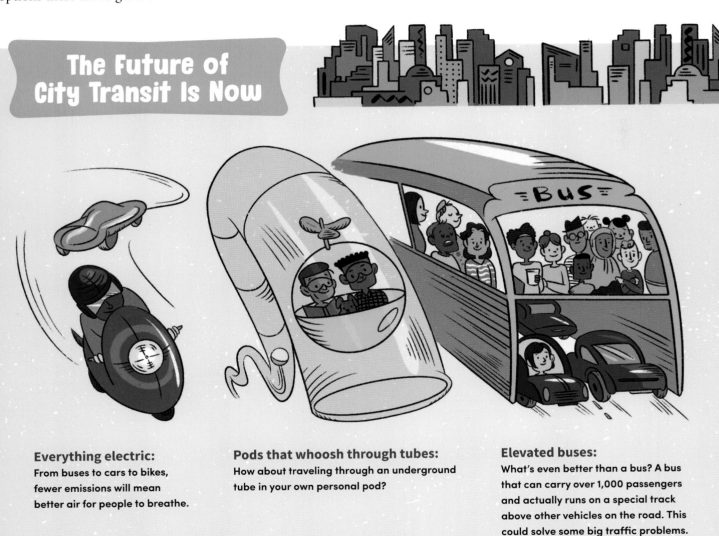

Everything electric:
From buses to cars to bikes, fewer emissions will mean better air for people to breathe.

Pods that whoosh through tubes:
How about traveling through an underground tube in your own personal pod?

Elevated buses:
What's even better than a bus? A bus that can carry over 1,000 passengers and actually runs on a special track above other vehicles on the road. This could solve some big traffic problems.

Xiangfen, China
2000 BCE

Rome
300

London, England
1870

Philadelphia
1700s

Three

Water and Waste

People can't live without water, even for a day, so all cities, right from the beginning, had to be near a source of clean drinking water. But where there are humans, there's also waste—guaranteed! Since germs love a crowd, city planners and engineers have had to figure out how to keep the water away from the waste. Sounds simple, right? Turns out it's not that easy. Unsafe water has often plagued residents of cities. Today water is in short supply in some places, including Cairo and Mexico City.

And what about garbage? In many places today you can put your garbage out for pickup or take it down to your building's dumpster, but what happens next? Cities through time have found ways to make treasure out of trash. Can we learn from the past how to deal with our waste in cities of today and tomorrow? Our planet sure hopes so. The good news is that humans are working on reducing, recycling and reusing everything. Yep, everything!

QUENCHING THIRST

Access to drinking water is a must-have for survival, whether you draw it from deep wells, capture it from rooftops or simply turn on the tap in your kitchen. As cities continue to grow, so does the demand for water. At the same time, the climate crisis has reduced water supply in many places. But ideas from the past might help us today, and the future of water is all about using it more than once.

Capturing Drops to Drink

Aqueducts: The Romans were famous for the channels they built to transport fresh water to cities, but *aqueducts* were built in many places, including Egypt, India and Turkey.

Rainwater harvesting: Historically, cities in Africa, Asia and the Americas collected rain and stored it in underground caverns or cisterns. Rainwater continues to be collected in cities in today around the world, often in aboveground storage tanks.

Dams and reservoirs: A dam is a structure built across a river to stop the flow of water. The water that collects behind the dam forms a lake, called a *reservoir*, which provides drinking water to cities, sometimes through pipes that stretch for many miles.

Germs Love a Crowd

In ancient times, you might draw water from a deep well lined with ceramic bricks, like they did in places such as Xiangfen, China. If the water was clear and smelled okay, you'd sip. Unless it tasted terrible, you'd likely consider it safe to drink. Although some cultures, including the ancient Greeks and the Chinese, suspected that water could spread disease and figured boiling it would be wise, the concept of invisible germs wouldn't be understood until thousands of years later.

In London, England, a cholera epidemic struck in 1854. At the time, people thought cholera was spread by bad air. But a local doctor named John Snow observed that people in one neighborhood got cholera while those only one block away didn't. His investigation found that the people with cholera had pumped water from a well contaminated with garbage. Dr. Snow had the handle removed from the well so that people could no longer use it, and the cholera outbreak was stopped.

Clean Water?

In 1806 the city of Paris used sand and charcoal to filter drinking water and remove solids such as human waste, but the main goal was to improve the look of the water. There was still a great debate about whether "foul" or "bad" air caused disease, or whether germs and *parasites* were the real culprits. In 1893 city officials in Hamburg added *chlorine*, a chemical disinfectant, to the public water supply. In 1908 Jersey City became the first city in the United States to use chlorine in its drinking water. Thousands of cities followed, and the number of typhoid and cholera cases plummeted.

While chlorine helped, many people in cities today still don't have safe drinking water. There's a lot of reasons why, including water being pumped through lead pipes or industrial chemicals leaching into the water supply. In the United States alone, more than 30 million people in 2020 got their water from systems that violate safety regulations. And in Canada in 2022, there were boil-water advisories in 29 communities, many of them Indigenous.

The Chand Baori stepwell was built around 800 CE in the Rajasthan state of India to provide water year-round in the desert climate, as well as a space to escape the daytime heat. It has 3,500 steps and 13 levels—phew!
MARC GUITARD/GETTY IMAGES

Not Enough Water? Try This

In 2015, São Paulo, Brazil, nearly ran out of water and was saved at the last minute by rainfall. The climate crisis has altered weather patterns, and cities can look to the past to engineer new ways to obtain and clean water.

Wastewater: Orange County in California, an area of 17 cities with 2.5 million people, recycles nearly all its *wastewater* and by 2023 will generate 130 million gallons (591 million liters) of drinking water a day.

Saltwater: More and more, cities are turning to ocean water for their drinking water. The problem is, you can't drink seawater unless you remove the salt in a process called *desalination*. Israel, one of the world's driest countries, depends on desalination for 80 percent of its drinking water. And in San Diego each day, 100 million gallons (455 million liters) of seawater create 50 million gallons (227 million liters) of drinking water.

Rainwater: The ancient practice of rain harvesting has returned to a number of cities, including Singapore, Bengaluru (India) and Mexico City. They all have programs to collect rainwater in tanks to use for drinking water and other household uses. And in São Paulo and Curitiba, Brazil, new buildings must have rainwater-harvesting systems.

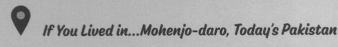

In ancient times (2500–1900 BCE), Mohenjo-daro was a vibrant city with as many as 100,000 residents at its height. The city had assembly halls, marketplaces, grain warehouses and plenty of bathhouses. Your parents might have been artisans who created jewelry from gold or lapis. One of your chores might have been to draw water from one of the 700 freshwater wells situated throughout the city. With so many wells, you likely had a short walk back with a heavy water container. If you had to "go"? You could head to the bathroom in your own home, where baked-clay drains carried waste away to sewers located below street level.

Archaeologists believe that the ancient city of Mohenjo-daro in modern-day Pakistan centered around the Great Bath, shown here in the middle of this photo. Keeping clean must have been top of mind for residents living here!
SAQIB QAYYUM/WIKIMEDIA COMMONS/ CC BY-SA 3.0

WATER IN, WASTE OUT

It's a fact—all humans need to drink water and eat food every day. But the flip side of that is they also need to go to the bathroom. Dealing with human waste is a stinky but necessary challenge for cities.

Ancient Toilets and Taps

Many ancient cities had wells nearby, indoor bathrooms and drainage systems that whisked away stinky sewage. Ancient Romans had public baths with multiple pools. By the fourth century it's believed that as many as 60,000 Romans could bathe at one time! The aqueducts provided Roman cities with fresh, clean running water that also carried waste away.

Piles of Poop

London in the 1300s reeked. But the smell wasn't the biggest problem.

Human waste was piling up. People built **cesspits**, but leaky ones caused trouble between neighbors. Night-soil men worked after dark to scoop human waste into carts and haul it out of town. People who couldn't afford their services tossed the contents of their **chamber pots** out their windows. The fine for tossing waste was two shillings, but catching perpetrators was tricky. Rats thrived, spreading diseases such as the deadly Black Plague, which killed as many as 25 million people in medieval Europe.

Wheeling Water Up

During the 1500s and 1600s in India, summer temperatures rose to 115 degrees Fahrenheit (46 degrees Celsius). Shahjahanabad (better known as Delhi) had a population of one million people. Surrounded by a large, deep moat filled with water from Yamuna River, the city had a system of canals, wells and reservoirs that provided water to thirsty residents. Toilets, some flushing, removed waste by gravity and took it through stone sewers to the moat. The Agra Fort, built for the Mughal rulers of the time, was located on the banks of the Yamuna River and surrounded by high walls. The walls were excellent for defense, but water doesn't run uphill. People solved this issue by raising water up over the walls using the Persian wheel system. A huge wooden wheel, heaved around by horses or bulls, lifted water 70 feet (21 meters) up and filled water tanks at the high points of the fort.

Sending Waste Down and Out of Town

Five thousand years ago, many cultures, including the Minoans (on what is now the Greek island of Crete), used sewage to help grow food. Later, in numerous cities in Europe, China and Japan, buckets of household waste were collected and sent out of town. This dealt with the mountains of city waste while providing valuable fertilizer for farmers' fields. Today some cities are transforming sewage into *biosolids*. Kansas City, Missouri, processes more than 70 million gallons of raw sewage a year into biosolids that are packed with nutrients for the corn and soybeans that farmers grow and sell to biofuel producers. Other cities repurpose waste in similar ways.

But there was another way to get rid of waste. In the mid-1800s, fed up with unsafe water and the stench of sewage, people started to build major sewer systems underground. By 1870 in London, they had constructed 82 miles (132 kilometers) of sewers using over 300 million bricks! Other cities followed suit, and with cleaner water and better waste removal, they started to become safer, more pleasant, less smelly places to live.

By the middle of the 19th century, the Chicago River was so polluted that city engineers reversed the course of the entire river, sending the sewage and pollution away from the city and bringing clean water to Chicago from Lake Michigan. The only problem? Cities downstream weren't too pleased.

CITY UNDERGROUND

When you walk on the sidewalk in your town or city, you are walking on top of a hidden world—a maze of pipes, tunnels and sewers. Without those things, our homes wouldn't have water, we would not be able to flush our toilets, and keeping the waste away from the water would be almost impossible.

Sewer Tour, Anyone?

In Paris in 1870, taking a boat tour of the sewers was a popular day trip. Keeping all the systems running was a big job for sewer inspectors. Gripping bright lights, they descended into the tunnels to search for problems such as clogged sewers or leaky pipes. Today's inspectors have technology such as cameras that slide into pipes to locate problems.

Watch Out for Alligators

The world underneath New York City descends almost 80 stories. Deep under the sidewalk, water and steam pipes twist and turn, turtles swim in the sewers, and an old ship, a six-lane highway and an entire grove of trees are buried in the depths of the underground world. Tales of alligators still raise eyebrows.

Rise Up for Sewers

In 1854 a cholera outbreak in Chicago killed one in 20 residents. The city decided it needed to build a sewer system under the existing buildings. In 1860, 600 laborers, working block by block, used jacks to raise shops, offices and hotels by six feet to make room for sewers to be installed underneath the buildings. It was a slow process, and city life went on as usual.

Do alligators live in the New York City sewers? Some people believe so, but no one can say for sure. In the 1930s purchasing baby alligators as pets became popular. Once they got too big to be considered cute, some may have been "released"—but where?
THE OLD MAJOR/SHUTTERSTOCK.COM

City Sewers by the Numbers

Philadelphia, early 1800s
45 miles (72 kilometers) of pipes made from pine logs.

Paris, 1870s
More than 300 miles (482 kilometers) of sewer tunnels under the city.

New York City, 2022
Over 7,400 miles (11,909 kilometers) of pipes.

Sewer tunnels and pipes come in many sizes. Some you can easily walk through, while others would be an impossible squeeze. They have been made of lead, cast iron, clay, concrete and even hollowed-out logs.
ATSUSHI FUJIKAWA / EYEEM/GETTY IMAGES

The City as a Forest

More than 50 percent of **Singapore** is devoted to parks and green spaces.

London has as many trees as people.

Chennai, India, plans to plant 1,000 mini-forests to absorb pollutants and reduce the temperature.

SOAKING UP THE STORM

If you've been out on a walk during a big storm, you might have noticed that rainwater falls onto the streets and sidewalks and then drops into drains. Eventually it flows into rivers and lakes. But streets and city buildings can be designed to both soak up the stormwater to reduce flooding and repurpose it so that we are getting the most out of each drop of rain. One study showed that if rainwater collection systems were installed in a number of cities, including Philadelphia, Seattle and Chicago, residents could capture anywhere from 21 to 75 percent of their non-drinking-water needs.

Rain gardens are sunken areas that collect rain from streets or other city surfaces and help to soak the water back into the ground, filtering out contaminants or debris before they reach our drinking water. This one is in my rainy hometown of North Vancouver, BC.
DAVE.CLENDENAN

Rainwater can also be collected in tanks and used to water gardens or, inside our homes, to flush toilets or wash dishes, saving precious drinking water. What could you do with the water you collect from the sky? Water your strawberries? Wash your clothes? Have a water fight?
DELOVELY PICS/SHUTTERSTOCK.COM

GARBAGE PITS

Ancient Minoa, part of today's Greece, had trash pits that were covered up with dirt. Archaeologists have found piles of discarded pottery in cities in ancient Rome and India, which they believe to be remnants of takeout food bowls. For most of history, people buried their garbage, tossed it in waterways or just left it in the streets. Today's garbage often contains old electronics, batteries, synthetic clothing and other materials full of toxic chemicals that are bad for both human health and our planet.

Hog Wild

In the 1700s in Philadelphia, hogs helped clean up the city's garbage. They roamed the streets, eating rotting food that had been thrown into the roads. In 1793 a yellow fever outbreak killed 5,000 people in the city (10 percent of the population). It was thought that cleaning the streets might help prevent the spread. It wasn't until 1881 that people understood yellow fever was caused by mosquitos. While people may not have understood their true cause, epidemics such as yellow fever helped spur cities to take more responsibility for cleaning their streets and removing garbage, things many people still benefit from today.

Burn It or Toss It

One way to get rid of rubbish is to burn it. The first **incinerator**, called the Destructor, was built in Nottingham, England, in 1874. Incinerators were built across North America in the 1900s. But burning garbage produces toxic fumes. In 1957 Los Angeles had to ban incinerators because the air was so polluted. Garbage dumps, also called *landfills*, have their own problems. They ooze toxic chemicals into the ground and release methane, a gas that contributes to the climate crisis. It is often the city's poorest residents who live near waste dumps and are exposed to toxic fumes.

Piggeries, small pig farms located in what is today's Central Park, dealt with some of New York City's food waste before there was city garbage collection. It took 75 pigs to eat about 2,000 pounds (907 kilograms) of food waste each day.

Meet Mr. Trash Wheel, a solar- and water-powered trash cleaner that collects litter and debris flowing into Baltimore's Inner Harbor.
ADAM LINDQUIST/WATERFRONT PARTNERSHIP OF BALTIMORE

Garbage Power

North America's largest landfill is the Apex Regional Landfill in Las Vegas, which receives 5 billion pounds (226,796 metric tons) of solid waste each year. Methane gas from the landfill generates enough energy to power 11,000 households. Other cities are burning garbage for power. Linköping, Sweden, burns garbage 24 hours a day to generate power for the city, a process known as waste-to-energy. While it diverts trash from landfills, it still creates pollution, so it's not a clean energy source. Pay-to-throw and waste-to-energy are a couple of new ways to manage city garbage. But do we need to produce so much garbage in the first place?

Tuned up to take your trash! While the musical trucks play a few different tunes, the most common piece played is Für Elise *by Beethoven.*
玄史生/WIKIMEDIA COMMONS/
PUBLIC DOMAIN

📍 If You Lived in...Taipei, Taiwan

It's 2023 in Taipei, and your ears perk up when music drifts through your window. It's the garbage truck, playing classical music to alert residents that it's time to take out the trash. You run to the kitchen to gather the trash and recycling, then head downstairs to the street. You throw the bags into the trucks yourself. A recycling truck follows the garbage truck. Often many people gather by the trucks, and you might have a chance to play with some neighbors. In Taipei garbage is not allowed to be placed on the ground or the curb. It must go directly into the garbage truck. It's a "pay-to-throw" system. That means there's a fee for the garbage bags that must be used, but recyclable and compostable items can be disposed of for free.

A SECOND CHANCE

Garbage or opportunity? We toss a lot, but many things can have a new life as something else! Before recycling bins or collection trucks, people often reused and repurposed rather than tossing their old items. In many cities, that's still the case. Almost everything in Cuba is reused, repurposed or repaired. If you hop in a taxi, you might sit on a seat cover made of old jeans, hiding the holes in the original material. If a door handle rusts off, it might be replaced with a loop of strong rope. If your fan or clock breaks, you find another broken one and combine the parts.

Sort and Salvage

In the 17th century, markets were held every morning at dawn in Edo, present-day Tokyo. Old clothing was sold to be reused as diapers, rags and other household items. This reflects an ancient Japanese concept called mottainai, meaning that each object we own should be valued and not simply discarded. This philosophy is still practiced today. At the 2020 Tokyo Olympics, medals were made out of recycled electronics donated by the public.

In 1854 London, England, was home to many people who made their living by collecting rags and metal to be repurposed. Without them, the city would have been crammed with waste. Although many cities today have recycling programs, many still don't. An estimated 15 to 20 million people make a living as **waste pickers**, in places such as Durban (South Africa), Manila (the Philippines) and Pune (India). Although they provide a valuable service, most waste pickers work in dangerous and unhealthy conditions.

Give Something, Get Something

In Bogotá, Colombia, reverse vending machines are found in shopping malls, public squares and schools. Deposit a plastic bottle, and you receive a gift such as movie tickets or restaurant coupons. The plastic collected by the machine is recycled. Similar machines are found in many other cities, including New Delhi and Beijing.

Treasure, Not Trash

Cairo 800s
Hemp ropes, fishing nets and old robes were transformed into paper.

London 1400s
Silver coins were melted down to make spoons.

New York City 1980s
Aluminum cans were collected and returned to make new cans.

Delhi 2020s
E-waste such as old phones is collected and repurposed.

Everything Gets Used Again

Tenochtitlán, Mexico, the capital of the Aztec world, found a new purpose for most of what we might consider waste. Food waste was fed to animals. Human waste was used as fertilizer, to tan leather or to create fabric dye. Other waste was burned. A number of cities today have set themselves the goal of creating zero waste. Vancouver, British Columbia, voted to do that by 2040.

Zero waste encourages a different way of thinking about resources. Today, most of the products we buy are produced, we use them, and when we are finished we throw them out or sometimes recycle them. But a zero-waste or *circular economy* aims to create products that can naturally be returned to the earth or reused many times or in a new way. What might this look like in a city?

- Transform food waste and wastewater into energy to heat homes or fertilizer for gardens.
- Share and repair everything, from furniture, clothes and toys to electronics and bicycles.
- Design waste-free products and packaging. Pass the compostable mushroom fork, please!
- Focus on reduce, reuse and finally, if the product cannot have another use, recycle.

No need to create more waste—there's a colorful recycling container for everything in Curitiba, Brazil.
ZAF/WIKIMEDIA COMMONS/CC BY-SA 3.0

Underground tubes: How about having your garbage and recycling sucked down a tube and recycled or burned for energy? Bonuses are less noise and smell, no trucks on the streets and fewer carbon dioxide emissions.

Portable clean water: How about a machine the size of a dishwasher that can run off energy from cow dung and purify water—even sewage water—so that it's pristine and clean? American inventor Dean Kamen has created just that.

Circular economy: What if every product you bought could be returned somewhere to be repurposed, reused or recycled? Goodbye, garbage!

Greece
400 BCE

China
400–200 BCE

Detroit
1800s

Glasgow
1887

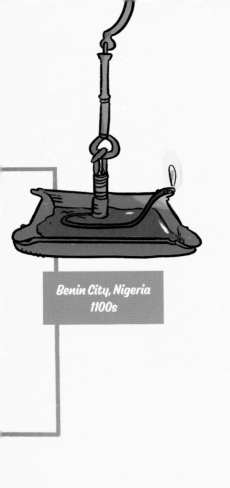

Benin City, Nigeria
1100s

Four
Lights,
Power,
Action!

Wellington,
New Zealand
2009

If you were to look at Earth from space today, you'd see the lights of thousands of cities. Streetlights brighten dark evenings. Homes and businesses are filled with televisions, microwaves, computers and other appliances. Hospitals use life-saving electrical equipment. Cities of the past got power from *renewable resources* like the sun's rays or water-powered mills. But cities today burn huge amounts of climate-changing fossil fuels such as coal and gas. People are seeking more sustainable ways of generating power and light, and some are looking to the past for ideas.

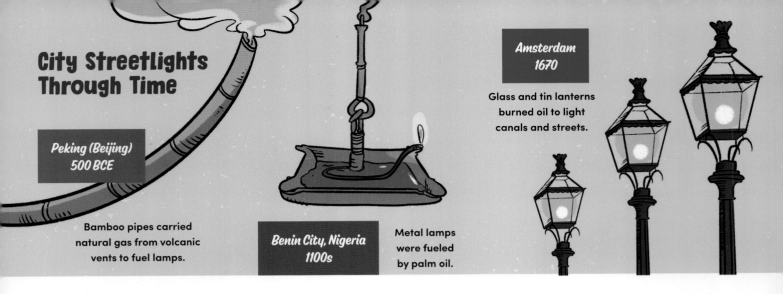

City Streetlights Through Time

Peking (Beijing)
500 BCE

Bamboo pipes carried natural gas from volcanic vents to fuel lamps.

Benin City, Nigeria
1100s

Metal lamps were fueled by palm oil.

Amsterdam
1670

Glass and tin lanterns burned oil to light canals and streets.

CITIES CAST A GLOW

Walking down a street with no lights might have been great for seeing the stars, but it sure wasn't easy to find your way around. Ancient Greeks carried clay dishes filled with olive oil, lit with a wick made of linen or papyrus. The lamps helped people find their way after dark. Inns and restaurants placed clay lamps outside their doors and along the streets to help people walk safely after sundown and to discourage thieves.

Cities have become so bright that many people are now looking at ways to reduce *light pollution.* It endangers animals whose life cycles depend on darkness, including humans' natural sleep and wake cycles.

Cities Brighten Up

In Geneva, during the Middle Ages, before streetlights existed, a curfew bell would ring to announce the end of the day. Everyone returned home to bolt their doors and shutter their windows. The city gates were locked to keep out intruders. Watchmen took turns patrolling the streets at night with a torch or lantern. Today most cities are well lit. And that's a good thing, because research has shown that brighter lights make people feel safer at night and more likely to go for a walk.

Moonlight Towers

In 1807 Sir Humphry Davy, an inventor, discovered that he could produce a blinding white light by connecting two charcoal rods to a battery. He called it an *arc lamp.* Hundreds of thousands of arc lamps were installed on streets in cities across Europe and North America. They were so bright that people sometimes used umbrellas to shield themselves from the glare. Entire city blocks were lit by arc lamps on towers that rose as high as 300 feet (90 meters). Cities were lit like sports stadiums. By 1890 Detroit had 122 moonlight towers that illuminated 21 square miles (54 square kilometers) of the city. Arc lamps were eventually replaced by other forms of electric light.

Time to Change the Light Bulbs

Electric streetlights now brighten up our cities, but they emit almost 2 million tons (1.8 metric tons) of greenhouse gases worldwide. So how about changing up the light bulbs? Buenos Aires, Argentina, replaced 91,000 streetlights with energy-efficient LED lights. Just this action reduced annual carbon dioxide emissions by 24,000 tons (21,772 metric tons) a year!

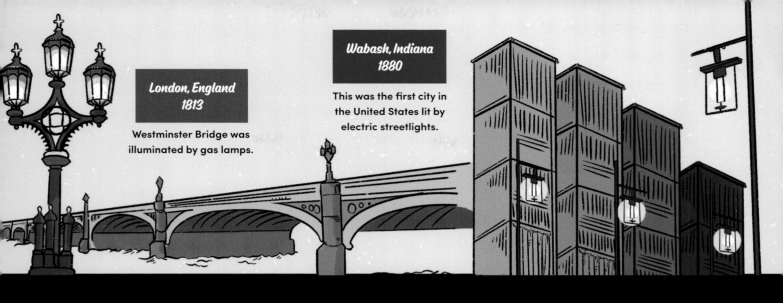

London, England 1813

Westminster Bridge was illuminated by gas lamps.

Wabash, Indiana 1880

This was the first city in the United States lit by electric streetlights.

If You Lived in...Paris, France

In 1667 the streets were unlit, and thieves were common. Eventually King Louis XIV demanded that streets be lit to reduce crime. So from November to March you had to place a candle or an oil lamp on your windowsill. By 1669 your street felt safe enough after dinner to play with your friends outside. Over time Paris began to dazzle with light. By 1857 the Grands Boulevards were ablaze at night, and people went out after dark. Each gaslight gave off about 10 candles' worth of power. By 1900 Paris had 50,900 streetlamps and is still known today as the City of Light.

The Pont Alexandre III spans the Seine River in Paris and features statues, carvings and elaborate lampposts. Walking across this bridge is like visiting an outdoor museum.
S-F/SHUTTERSTOCK.COM

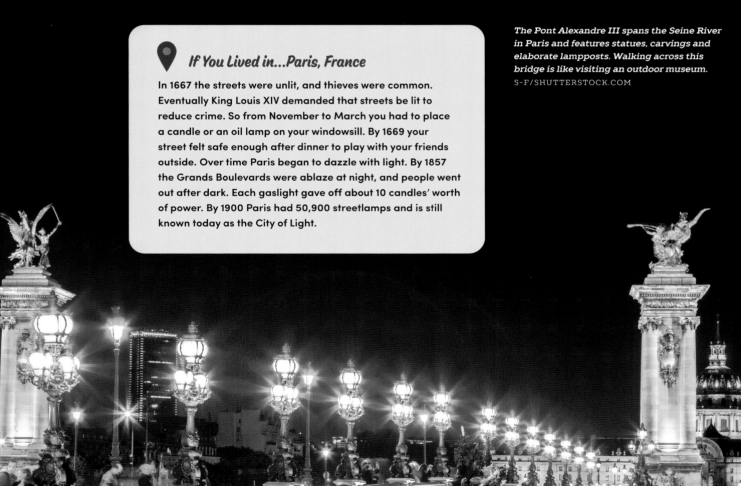

ELECTRIC BUZZ

On September 4, 1882, the Edison Illuminating Company, headed by inventor and businessman Thomas Edison, lit up parts of lower Manhattan for the first time with electric *incandescent* light. Electric lights were now inside, not just outside as arc lamps were. New York City became famous for its brightly lit theaters, restaurants and concert halls. People who worked during the day could now enjoy a night out after dark, but other people ended up working longer hours in well-lit factories. At first some people were suspicious of indoor electric lights, believing they could cause headaches, eyestrain or even freckles! Electricity didn't just light up cities—it changed how they were built.

Going Up!

Every night in Shanghai the skyscrapers of the Pudong district light up with the colors of the rainbow. The skyscrapers of today, with elevators, lights, heating and power for thousands of computers and appliances, require a lot of electricity! We might not think too much about stepping into an elevator these days, but before 1854 elevators couldn't always stop safely. That year Elisha Otis and his sons invented an elevator safety brake. With this advanced technology, buildings could be much taller. Skyscrapers became popular in cities worldwide, as people liked the views as well as living farther from street noise.

Skyscrapers Stretch High

12 STORIES

31 STORIES

101 STORIES

102 STORIES

163 STORIES

1885
Home Insurance Building
Chicago

1889
Park Row Building
New York City

2004
Taipei 101
Taipei, Taiwan

1931
Empire State Building
New York City

2010
Burj Khalifa
Dubai

Switching On

With indoor electric lights, factories could operate around the clock, extending the workday for many people. In private residences, when electricity was first introduced, only wealthy families could afford to have it. The first home wired for electricity was J.P. Morgan's in New York City, in June 1882. It required an engineer to come each day from 3 p.m. to 11 p.m. By 1920 electricity was available to 35 percent of urban homes in the United States. But poor neighborhoods mostly remained in the dark for many more years to come.

Powering Off

On November 9, 1965, 30 million people in the US northeast and Ontario lost power. It was evening, and many people were headed home from work in elevators, trains and cars. In New York alone, 800,000 people were trapped in the subway. Doctors performed surgeries by flashlight. Airports lost radar and planes couldn't land. At the Bronx Zoo, small portable gas heaters were brought in to keep the vipers, iguanas and crocodiles warm. The power was restored by the next day, but the experience helped people realize how much they depended on electricity and that they needed to have plans in place for when they lost power.

BIG FOOTPRINTS

Cities are lit up and open for business 24 hours a day. But where does all the power come from? Early cities relied on energy from the sun, rushing water and fire. But after the Industrial Revolution, there was a shift to burning fossil fuels like coal, oil and gas. Cities today consume over two-thirds of the world's energy and are responsible for more than 60 percent of global greenhouse gas emissions, which are a major contributor to the climate crisis.

Warming Toes

Fireplaces, also called hearths, have warmed many cold toes in homes, castles, restaurants and other public places around the world. But fire creates smoke. In Korea, from about 1000 BCE to the 1960s, people built under-floor heating systems called ondols. A wood fire burned under a stone floor that absorbed the heat and brought warmth to the room without smoke. Today modern ondol floors in Korea are heated by water instead of fire, but they still create cozy spaces.

Belching Black Smoke

Wood burned nicely, but by the late 1500s, the forests near London were dwindling. A new heat source was needed, and that's where coal came in. Coal is a type of black rock that is found underground and can be burned like wood. By the 1600s coal was burned in most London homes, and by the 1700s ships filled with coal sailed into London, ready to power its many factories. Burning coal is a stinky, dirty process that releases toxic pollutants harmful to human health. But coal is also an inexpensive source of fuel, and many cities still use coal for power. Today, nine out of 10 people on the planet breathe polluted air.

Water Power

From 400 to 200 BCE, people in Egypt, China and Greece were finding ways to use water as a powerful source of energy. A water wheel with paddles used the flow of a river or waterfall to create energy. The power created moved whatever was attached to the wheel, such as a mill to hull rice. Now people could put their feet up and let technology do at least some of their work! In medieval Europe, a water-powered mill could grind enough flour to feed the town, and it could also be used to prepare wool or saw wood.

In 1895 Buffalo, New York, was powered by electricity sent through transmission lines from Niagara Falls, where 3,160 tons (2,866 metric tons) of water flows over the falls every second.

Today huge *hydroelectric* dams supply power to cities around the world. While hydroelectric power is a renewable energy source because it uses the power of running water, building the reservoirs to hold the water can flood local communities and harm animal habitats.

Power Up, Pollution Down

Burning fossil fuels for city power has come at a big cost to both our health and our planet. Some researchers believe that if everyone works together, it's possible for our world to change back to renewable energy sources by 2050. Cities of the past used the power of the sun and the wind—can we do the same in the future?

BLOWING IN THE WIND

When the wind blows hard, it can knock down everything in its path. Why not harness that power for good? Humans have been using wind power for centuries. Iran, the Netherlands, China, England and many other countries used windmills to grind grain, saw wood or pump water for their crops. In 1887 Professor James Blyth of Glasgow built the first electricity-producing wind turbine—some say he powered his own house for 25 years with his final design!

More and more, cities are using wind to create electricity. It's a renewable energy source that does not produce greenhouse gas emissions or pollution. Turbines as tall as a 20-story building, with 200-foot (60-meter) blades, convert the wind that passes through spinning blades into electrical energy that can be transported to cities via transmission lines. Wind farms do have downsides. They require a lot of space and materials. They can also injure or even kill birds and bats, as well as disrupt their flight paths.

World's Windiest City

Wellington, New Zealand, sits on the edge of the Cook Strait, where the wind whips in across thousands of miles of ocean. Sixty-two turbines on a wind farm operated by Meridian Energy, located 4.5 miles (7.5 kilometers) from the city center, generate enough electricity each year to power 70,000 homes. Wellington is just one of many cities around the world that are catching the wind to power up.

Wind turbines generate electricity behind a residential neighborhood near Wellington, New Zealand.
CHAMELEONSEYE/SHUTTERSTOCK.COM

Rooftop Wind Power

Fitting huge turbines with rotating blades into already crowded cities is tricky. Scientists have developed small wind turbines that can be placed on building roofs, bridges and even streetlights. They don't provide as much power as large wind farms do, but they take up less space and pose less of a threat to birds and bats. In 2008 the World Trade Center in Bahrain was the first skyscraper to be built with its own wind turbines. They supply up to 15 percent of the building's electrical energy needs. In Paris, the Eiffel Tower now sports two wind turbines, located inside on the second level, about 400 feet (122 meters) above ground. And in London, England, and Guangzhou, China, large skyscrapers with built-in wind turbines generate their own energy.

Wind turbines on the World Trade Center in Bahrain.
TRABANTOS/GETTY IMAGES

Cooling Breezes

As the climate crisis heats up cities worldwide, more people are turning up the air-conditioning to stay comfortable and cool. But that's heating up our planet, because air conditioners emit greenhouse gases. For centuries in hot, dry places such as Iran and Egypt, people took advantage of desert breezes to create a natural cooling system called a wind tower. This tall, chimney-shaped structure is located on top of buildings. Inside the tower, air heats up and then rises. As the warm air passes out the top, it draws in cooler breezes. The cooler air travels down the chimney and into the building. Wind towers require no energy and produce no pollution. When air-conditioning was invented, the towers became less common, but as the costs of air-conditioning rise, people are looking back to wind towers to help cool cities. Today Masdar City in the United Arab Emirates has a 147-foot (45-meter) wind tower that helps cool the surrounding city streets by up to 9 degrees Fahrenheit (5 degrees Celsius).

People enjoying the warm waters of Blue Lagoon in Iceland, which is heated by geothermal energy.
TIM E. WHITE/GETTY IMAGES

 ### If You Lived in...Reykjavik, Iceland

In today's Reykjavik, your home would be warmed by under-your-feet heat. Iceland, an island country, has snow-capped mountains and hundreds of volcanoes and hot springs. It's also at the boundary of two *tectonic plates*. They bump against each other and bring the heat closer to the surface. All this action means that Iceland bubbles up an almost limitless source of hot water, called *geothermal energy*. Geothermal energy can be used to produce electricity, heat buildings and swimming pools, and even melt snow from sidewalks so people don't slip. Tap water in Iceland is pumped from hot springs.

HERE COMES THE SUN

The sun shines down on Earth every minute of every day with enough energy to potentially power all human activities. Using the heat of the sun isn't a new idea. It's a renewable resource, costs less money in the long run than other energy sources and doesn't create emissions. Now that's a bright idea.

Solar Energy

In ancient times people used clay and stone walls to trap heat from the sun during the day and slowly release it at night. Ancient Chinese buildings were often built with only one opening, which faced south to take advantage of the sun and keep out the cold northern winds. City planners designed the main streets of Chinese cities to run east to west, allowing every house to catch the winter sun's heat. Today architects create walls of glass to let in the sun, paired with heat-absorbing material such as bricks, stone or concrete. A *passive solar house* is designed so that the sun heats the home and provides daytime lighting, and wind cools the home.

Want to cool your building or home without air-conditioning? Try painting the roof white! Many city buildings have a coat of white paint to help reflect or absorb sunlight and reduce the urban-heat-island effect.

SOURCE: THE UNITED STATES DEPARTMENT OF ENERGY

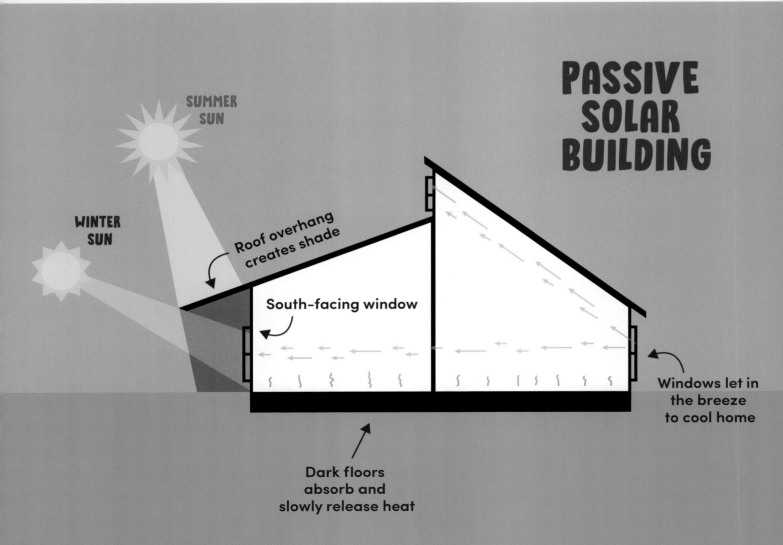

PASSIVE SOLAR BUILDING

SUMMER SUN

WINTER SUN

Roof overhang creates shade

South-facing window

Windows let in the breeze to cool home

Dark floors absorb and slowly release heat

Solar Panels

Solar panels capture the sun's energy and generate electricity. In Adelaide, Australia, population 1.3 million, sun and wind power many city facilities, including an aquatic center, the town hall, a shopping center, a bus station and even street and traffic lights. The solar panels are reducing carbon dioxide emissions in the city by 838 tons (760 metric tons) of carbon dioxide each year, which is like taking 302 gas-powered cars off the road.

Cape Town, South Africa, relies on coal energy, but they are trying to make a change. The city encourages its residents to install solar panels on their roofs. If the solar panel you put on your roof generates more energy than you use, you can sell back the "extra" electricity for credit. Other cities, including San Diego and Ota City (Japan), have installed solar panels on the roofs of schools, hospitals and recreation centers to generate electricity for the community. And in Berlin, as of January 2023, all new buildings had to install solar panels on the roof.

Solar panels stretch across a roof in Bangkok, yet another city working to power up from the sun.
AMPOL KAENCHAIYAPHOOM/
SHUTTERSTOCK.COM

These five exhaust stacks of a plant in Vancouver, BC, that generates energy from sewage are topped with LED lights that change color to indicate energy demand.
CITY OF VANCOUVER

ROUND AND ROUND WE GO

In nature, nothing is wasted. Everything is reused, repurposed or recycled. Cities can learn from nature to create power and clean water in a circular system that means all resources move in a constant cycle with no waste.

Dig Down to Heat Up

For the 2010 Winter Olympics in Vancouver, British Columbia, the city needed a warm, cozy place for visiting athletes and for the 16,000 people who would live there after the games were over. As you read in chapter 3, underneath most cities today is a network of sewers that push waste from our toilets to wastewater treatment plants. Sewage generates a lot of heat. Vancouver designed a system that would recover the heat from untreated wastewater to power up the Olympic Village. Capturing heat from the sewers now provides about 70 percent of the neighborhood's annual energy and has reduced carbon emissions by about 50 percent.

Waste not, want not: City power in the future won't come from one renewable source but from many that work together. Wind, water and solar power will be stored and shared among networks of cities so that "extra" power is not wasted.

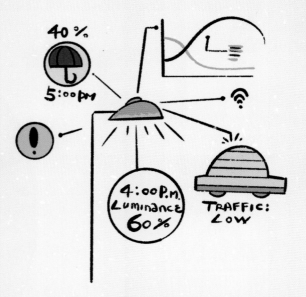

Lit up like nature: How about streetlights and road markings lit by natural compounds instead of chemicals or emissions? This idea is inspired by fireflies, jellyfish and certain types of mushrooms that naturally produce light called *bioluminescence*.

Smart streetlights: As well as providing light, streetlights will have cameras and sensors to manage traffic, monitor weather and air quality, or even provide automatic emergency response when accidents or crimes occur.

Uruk, Mesopotamia
1900 BCE

Rotterdam,
Netherlands
2019

Tenochtitlán
present-day
Mexico City
1400s

Five
Finding
Food

What's for dinner? Our stomachs remind us that we need to eat every day. And not just any food will do. To stay healthy, we need nutritious food like fresh fruit and vegetables. Ancient cities were often surrounded by fields where people grew food such as wheat, barley or rice. Chickens, pigs and cows were raised in the city. Markets brought farmers and city dwellers together. In many cities today, that's still the case. But in most, food has been transported huge distances. As cities grow and the climate crisis heats up our environment, farmers, businesses and citizens are looking at how cities of the past grew food and raised animals right in their centers. Can we learn from the past to get today's dinner on the table?

Paris
1870s

THE CITY AS FARM

What came first, the city or the farm? Researchers are still pondering this riddle, but we do know that the first cities were established in the same places as early farming. In Uruk, Mesopotamia, one of the world's first cities, thousands of hectares of fields growing wheat, barley and dates surrounded the city. Gardens produced fruit, herbs and vegetables.

Floating Gardens

In the 1400s in Tenochtitlán, located on the site of present-day Mexico City, the Aztecs built a system of floating gardens called *chinampas* in the lakes and canals surrounding the city. These island plots produced three crops a year, including beans, corn and squash. They grew at least 50 percent of the food consumed by the city's 200,000 residents.

Peaches in Paris

In 1870s Paris there were 372 miles (600 kilometers) of fruit walls that produced 17 million peaches a year. The massive stone walls stored heat from the sun and raised temperatures by as much as 18 degrees Fahrenheit (10 degrees Celsius) at night—perfect for growing peaches! In the central courtyard between these walls it was a bit chillier, but that worked well for growing crops better suited to cooler temperatures, including apples, pears and raspberries. The maze of jumbled fruit walls was so confusing that the Prussian army went around them during the siege of Paris in 1870.

Today the average North American strawberry might travel more than 2,000 miles (3,218 kilometers) by truck to reach a grocery store. But a strawberry grown in a city farm likely travels less than 10 miles (16 kilometers).

Cities Lend Some Land

If you live in a city but don't own land, how can you grow food? In the late 1800s, as more factory workers moved to cities, small plots of land in and near the city, called *allotments*, were given to people to grow their own food. In London, Paris, Berlin and Stockholm, allotments helped city residents grow healthy food they might otherwise not have been able to access or afford. By the 1930s, unemployed workers in the United States were loaned plots of land, and charities and the government helped with seeds and supplies so that people could grow their own food. During World Wars I and II, people planted Victory Gardens to help increase food production in cities across the world. In Chicago alone during World War II there were 33,000 gardens, covering nearly 1,800 acres (7.2 square kilometers).

How about taking science class in your school garden? Martin Luther King Jr. Middle School in Berkeley, CA, has run the Edible Schoolyard Project since 1995. Students learn about gardening and cooking and eat the food they grow.

Community gardens like this one in Turin, Italy, bring people together to build social connections, access healthy food and experience joy on a sunny afternoon.
MIKEDOTTA/SHUTTERSTOCK.COM

ANIMALS EVERYWHERE

Cows out front, pigs in the garden, chickens in a backyard—animals raised for milk, eggs or meat used to be everywhere in the city, in any city! Before refrigerators, fresh food such as milk spoiled quickly, and if people in the city didn't have a way to keep food cold, they had to be able to access it daily. In the 1800s you could find cows, pigs and chickens on the streets of Toronto, Montreal and Winnipeg, among other Canadian and American cities. While these animals are now banned or strictly limited in many cities, in others they remain part of life. Nairobi, Kenya, population 3.4 million, has over one million animals. Chickens, rabbits, goats, pigs and cows provide eggs, milk and meat. One-third to half of the fresh foods people eat are grown or raised in the city. Worldwide, millions of city residents raise animals for meat and eggs.

Horses Help Out

As horses clattered through the streets, they left piles of stinky manure—the perfect fertilizer for growing vegetables. In Paris in the 1800s there were market gardens, which were small farms that grew vegetables and fruits in suburban areas around the city. Poop from the city's many horses was dried and sold to the market gardeners to grow their vegetables. And wow, did these gardens ever grow! They were able to supply the entire city with vegetables, growing more than 100,000 tons (90,718 metric tons) per year. By the late 1800s, every person in Paris could have eaten 110 pounds (50 kilograms) of salad crops each year.

Your Dinner Grazed and Roamed

In the 1800s cows grazed in Boston and Winnipeg, and in New York City in the 1820s there were as many as 20,000 pigs.

At the time, the city population was growing rapidly and nearby farmland was being built over with shops, homes and factories. People still kept pigs—but they weren't pets. They needed them as a food source. Since they had nowhere else to put them, they left them in the streets. Pigs are great at eating food waste!

Rounding Up the Cows

Not everyone in the city loved the free-roaming pigs and cows. Wealthier city residents didn't like sharing space with animals. Others felt that the animals were the cause of epidemics such as cholera (they were wrong!). In New York in 1849, police rounded up thousands of pigs. In 1892 Montreal police impounded more than 800 animals, including horses, sheep, cows and pigs.

Besides the animals that people kept for their own use, slaughterhouses, piggeries and dairies of the time were crowded, stinky and producing waste that tainted drinking water. By the early to mid-1900s, farm animals were banned in many North American cities, including Baltimore, Boston, Philadelphia and New York, because people believed that removing animals would help keep the city clean. The line between farm and city became more divided. Today cities are creating new bylaws that allow chickens, pigs, bees and other small livestock to return to the city, but this time around, they won't be free-roaming.

City Farms

Seattle, United States:
Miniature goats, pot-bellied pigs, chickens and bees can be kept in backyards.

Toronto, Canada:
Cows, horses, pigs, goats and sheep live on a farm in the middle of the city.

Kampala, Uganda:
City households keep chickens and pigs, and cows for milk.

If You Lived in...
Havana, Cuba

In the 1990s in Havana, shops ran out of food to sell because Cuba's main trading partner, Russia, then known as the USSR, stopped sending food. To survive, you helped your family dig into every available patch of soil. You planted tomatoes in pots on your patio or lettuce in a nearby park. You might have tended chickens in your garage. Your family likely rolled up their sleeves and contributed to larger gardens in public places, called huertos. All your hard work paid off. By 1995 food was easier to find, as most was grown locally. Today about 90 percent of the fruits and vegetables eaten in Havana is still grown in the city.

MAKING SPACE TO GROW

While it's true that cities can't grow all their food (it's hard to squeeze in enough wheat fields or rice paddies in the middle of a city!), it is possible to find space to plant fruit trees, vegetable gardens and rooftop farms. Community gardens are places to meet neighbors, get outside and dig into the soil, and access nutritious food like fresh garden peas or carrots. Cities today can take some lessons from cities of the past by turning unused land into gardens and giving more people the space to grow their own food. In Mexico City, local farmers are reviving the chinampas (floating gardens) to help feed the growing population.

Can We Share?

Like the allotment gardens of the past, cities today are sharing space to give more people the opportunity to grow food. During the COVID-19 pandemic, people in Chiang Mai, Thailand, created an urban farm on a former landfill site and allowed people who had lost their jobs to grow food for themselves. In vacant lots in cities including Chicago and New York, people have created community gardens. In Saskatoon, farmers rent or borrow city backyards from homeowners to grow crops like lettuce and radishes and then sell the produce in weekly boxes or at farmers' markets. These projects also fight *food insecurity* by producing healthy vegetables at lower prices.

Homegrown to Sell

In Mumbai, people grow food in gardens on balconies to have a source of fresh fruits and vegetables, sometimes generating income by selling what's left over. Of the estimated 800 million urban farmers worldwide, the majority are women. They grow food both to feed their families and to earn a living. In Cotonou and Porto-Novo, Benin, allotment gardens are provided for women. They produce a variety of nutritious crops that are both eaten at home and sold.

Farming Up High and Down Low

If you were to look at a satellite image of a city and take note of all the roofs, you'd realize how much potential space there is to grow vegetables and fruit. In 2010 a company called Brooklyn Grange lifted 1.2 million pounds (544,311 kilograms) of soil onto the roof of a three-story warehouse in Brooklyn. Seeds were planted and cared for. That year the rooftop farm produced 15,000 pounds (6,804 kilograms) of fruit and vegetables. Today the company produces over 100,000 pounds (45,359 kilograms) of produce a year on three separate rooftops. And what about if we look underground for space? In Tokyo the company that operates the subway now grows salad greens and herbs in a facility under the elevated train tracks of the Metro Tozai Line.

Since 2008 Mexico City has installed 226,000 square feet (20,996 square meters) of rooftop gardens.

Any empty space in a city could be transformed into a delicious garden.
HAIREENA/SHUTTERSTOCK.COM

Founded in the 11th century, the Djemaa el Fna Market in Marrakech, Morocco, is a place where food sellers, musicians and artists gather each day. Grab some dinner at a stall and prepare to be entertained!

TO MARKET, TO MARKET

If you don't grow food, where do you buy it? Before there were grocery stores, there were markets. If you lived in ancient Athens, you'd shop for dinner at a bustling market, walking between clusters of stalls that sold fish, vegetables and meat. In Baghdad in the 700s, you could pick up figs and pastries, cardamom and pepper, even watermelon packed in snow. City markets were and are the center of many communities, providing not only fresh food each day but also a place to meet neighbors and sometimes the farmers who grew or raised the food.

In the United States today, more than 19 million people live in a *food desert*, an area where people have difficulty accessing affordable and fresh healthy food, especially fruits and vegetables.

Closing Shops, Opening Superstores

In the 1800s in New Orleans, everyone lived within walking distance of a market. Produce, meat and dairy were kept on ice, and customers came early, before it melted. In the 1940s cars became popular. Instead of purchasing fresh food daily, more people drove their cars to larger supermarkets farther away to buy a week's worth of groceries. Many of New Orleans' public markets closed. This happened in many cities across North America. If you didn't have a car, accessing food became more difficult. Today's local farmers' markets are returning to cities where they had previously closed down, as people seek food grown closer to home.

STREET FOOD

From fried fish in Athens to fruit tamales in Tenochtitlán to pad thai noodles in Bangkok, *street food* is ready-to-eat fare sold from small stalls or trucks in public spaces. Street food is prepared quickly and is inexpensive compared to restaurant fare. Selling it provides income to many people, but being a street vendor is hard work. Many work all day with no breaks and no bathroom nearby.

City Eating without a Kitchen

In ancient Rome many apartments had no kitchens, so people bought meals from street vendors. This was the case in many cities throughout history. Some of the offerings included wheat pounded into porridge, chickpea stew or bread with cheese and honey. In the 1200s in Angkor, in today's Cambodia, food vendors prepared cauldrons of soup and skewers of meat grilled over open flames.

A street vendor in Bangkok serves up satay and other delicious delights.
DAVID KUCERA/SHUTTERSTOCK.COM

Grab-and-Go City Foods

Nairobi, Kenya:
mandazi (a Kenyan doughnut),
roasted peanuts

Mumbai, India:
vada pav,
a deep-fried potato
dumpling in a bread bun

Portland, Oregon:
ramen noodles, kebabs,
Thai chicken

Meals for Millions

Today food stalls offer millions of meals every day to people who rely on street food as they work long hours far from home. Street vendors can move around the city and provide food in areas that don't have other restaurants. In Dhaka, Bangladesh, a city of 20 million people, more than 200,000 street vendors provide meals every day, including jhalmuri (puffed rice and vegetables) and samucha/ samosa (deep-fried dough stuffed with vegetables or meat). In Los Angeles there are more than 3,000 food trucks selling street food of all kinds.

 If You Lived in...Lagos, Nigeria

Your city streets are filled with packed cars and minibuses. Thousands of vendors sell a soft bread called agege, baked in the hundreds of local bakeries and distributed to sellers bright and early each day. Served with butter or mayonnaise, it's a quick breakfast meal for hungry commuters. For many people, grilled corn can't be beat as a tasty quick meal, and thousands of corn-roasting stalls line the roads.

In Lagos, corn is in season from August to November each year. Whether it's roasted or boiled, you don't want to miss out on this scrumptious snack.
I_AM_ZEWS/SHUTTERSTOCK.COM

Is this what farms will look like in the future?
ITSANAN SAMPUNTARAT/GETTY IMAGES

FEEDING BIGGER CROWDS

As cities continue to grow, the demand for food also grows. At the same time, the climate crisis is causing droughts, floods and other major weather events that affect the food supply. Cities are meeting these challenges by looking to the past and thinking outside the garden box.

Indoor Farming

Inside warehouses, under bright lights, stacks of green vegetables grow without soil, sunlight or seasons. Vertical indoor farms use less water compared to regular farms, require no pesticides and grow crops about 30 percent faster than in outdoor fields. They are also sheltered from extreme weather and can be located right in the middle of a city. Vertical farms are popping up in cities around the world.

The Cows Come Home

Rotterdam, Netherlands, is home to the world's first floating dairy farm, a three-story structure located in the middle of one of Europe's busiest ports. Milking stations are on the lower deck, and the cows live on the top floor. They can wander down a ramp onto a field on the shore next to their floating home to feed on discarded grass clippings from local fields and golf courses. No matter how much rain falls or how high the sea, the farm is designed to move up and down with the water levels.

Vertical Farming

Kameoka Farm near Kyoto produces up to 21,000 lettuce heads per day.

Sky Greens in Singapore harvests 1,764 pounds (800 kilograms) of leafy vegetables daily.

AeroFarms in Newark, New Jersey, grows more than 1,984,160 pounds (900,000 kilograms) of leafy greens each year.

Fish That Clean the Water

In Kolkata, India, a fish farmer named Bidu Sarkar made an unexpected discovery. After accidentally allowing untreated wastewater from Kolkata's sewage pipes into his fish pond, he expected his fish would die. But the opposite happened. He got twice as many fish. The hot Kolkata sunshine decomposed the sewage and allowed *plankton*, which the fish feed on, to thrive and grow. More than 50,000 fish farmers and traders today make a living raising fish in wastewater on the east side of Kolkata. At the same time, they are helping the city clean its wastewater. Other cities in Bangladesh, Pakistan, Thailand, Germany and France are now following the Kolkata model.

Feeding Ourselves, Preserving Our Planet

Imagine if you could walk down your street to a local store or market to purchase fruit grown near your home, or visit your community garden and harvest vegetables your family had grown. You may already be able to do this, but many people can't. And everyone needs access to healthy and affordable food. In Belo Horizonte, Brazil, food insecurity was a real problem. Many people were hungry and malnourished. To solve the problem, the city decided that food was a human right and, in 1993, created programs to feed everyone. They connected city people with nutritious food while at the same time supporting local urban farmers.

The Future of City Food Is Now

Everything is edible: How about replacing grass lawns with edible plants? In Davis, California, an area of homes surrounded by edible plants provides food for over 225 households.

Underground farming: There's a lot of room underneath cities to grow food. Paris is already growing mushrooms, endives and microgreens in unused underground parking lots.

Lab food: How about a *bacteria*-fermented pancake or a lab-grown burger? With limited space to farm, Singapore already allows the production and sale of lab-grown meat.

Imagine the City You'd Like to Call Home

Life in the city has changed over time, but what hasn't changed is people's ability to adapt to new situations, learn from the past, create new technology, cooperate with neighbors and find new ways to live together. If you could design a city that would be good for both people and the planet and treat all residents equitably, what would it look like?

Build upward to house more people. Link skyscrapers by sky bridges full of plants, rooftop farms and playgrounds.

Create public space for social connections that welcome all people.

Plan for people. Build complete, mixed-use neighborhoods to help people get around without cars.

Bring on more buses, separate bicycle lanes and safe sidewalks.

Build parks and places for every person and every creature, in all neighborhoods.

Learn from nature. Green infrastructure allows nature to help cities stay cool and absorbs water to reduce flooding.

Cut emissions. Power up with wind, water and solar energy.

Waste nothing. Recapture heat from sewage, recycle water, go zero waste.

Farm the city. Grow vegetables on the roof. Keep chickens at city hall.

Thousands of people enjoy Bryant Park in New York City, where you can picnic, play ball, visit with friends or ride a carousel. The park also provides chess, table tennis, a putting green, art supplies and so many other fun activities—for free!

DRAZEN_/GETTY IMAGES

Glossary

aqueducts—pipes, canals and tunnels used to transport fresh water

bacteria—tiny, single-celled organisms, found in all environments, that can be dangerous or beneficial

bioluminescence—light produced by a chemical reaction within a living organism, such as anglerfish, fireflies, jellyfish and fungi

biosolids—nutrient-rich material obtained from treating wastewater, often used as a natural fertilizer for growing food

braille—a reading and writing system for visually impaired people that uses patterns of raised dots representing letters that are read by touch

cesspits—holes or tanks in the ground for disposing of wastewater and sewage

chamber pot—a bowl that served as a portable toilet before there was indoor plumbing and flush toilets

chlorine—a chemical element with multiple uses, such as disinfecting drinking water and killing bacteria in swimming pools

cholera—an infectious disease caused by a type of bacteria that usually spreads through contaminated water

circular economy—an economic system in which waste is reduced and materials are repurposed, repaired or reused rather than disposed of, whenever possible

city planners—people who plan and design the ways that land, space and services within cities and towns will be used. Also known as urban planners

climate crisis—the effect of long-term shifts in global and regional weather and climate patterns, caused primarily by the burning of fossil fuels. Often used in reference to the rise in global temperatures from the mid- to late 1900s to today.

coal—a type of fossil fuel found underground, formed from the decomposition of plants or animals. It is a hard, black substance that can be burned to produce heat or power.

commute—travel on a regular basis between work or school and home

democracy—a form of government in which citizens can take part in how the government is run by voting for a leader and/or a representative

desalination—the process of removing salt and other minerals from water to make it drinkable for humans or animals, or to be used for soil in agriculture. The process uses significant fossil fuels, so it is usually done only in areas with little other choice for drinking water.

emissions—substances released into the air, such as exhaust from a car or gases from power plants and factories

feng shui—a Chinese practice of arranging and designing buildings and objects to achieve harmony and balance

food desert—an area where it is difficult for people to access affordable, healthy food, especially fruits and vegetables, because of a lack of stores, lack of transportation or high prices

food insecurity—the lack of regular access to enough food to sustain a healthy life

fossil fuels—fuels formed from the remains of plants and animals that were converted to oil, coal or natural gas by heat and pressure in the earth's crust over hundreds of millions of years

fractal—a pattern that repeats the same structure or shape, and every part resembles the larger structure. Fractal patterns in nature include snowflakes, tree branches and lighting bolts.

freeways—wide roads for fast-moving traffic, usually with few intersections and a limited number of places where drivers can enter and exit

gentrification—the altering of a city neighborhood by middle-class or wealthy people, which often results in displacement of current residents and businesses because they can no longer afford to live there

geothermal energy—heat produced through the decay of radioactive particles in the earth's core. Evidence of this is found in places with volcanic activity and natural hot springs. It's a renewable energy source.

hydroelectric—relating to the generation of power by the movement of water, such as a river. The pressure of the water turns a turbine, which powers a generator that creates electricity.

incandescent—a type of light produced when a thin piece of metal called a filament is heated by an electric current

incinerator—a furnace or machine for burning garbage, especially industrial waste, at high temperatures until it is reduced to ash

Industrial Revolution—a period in history marked by a shift from making things by hand in shops and homes to using power-driven machines in factories

light pollution—unwanted or excessive artificial light caused by streetlights and other human-made sources, which reduces the visibility of stars and other celestial objects and disrupts the natural cycles of many animals

living street—a street designed to be shared by pedestrians, cyclists and motorists but with right-of-way given to pedestrians. The concept of the living street, or woonerf, started in Delft, Netherlands, in the 1960s in response to an increase in cars in the city.

natural infrastructure—nature-based solutions to reduce the damaging effects of such things as erosion and flooding

parasites—organisms such as fleas, worms and fungi that live on or inside other living things in order to obtain food, grow or multiply, often causing harm to the host

passive solar house—a house that collects and distributes heat from the sun through the design and placement of windows, walls and floors, keeping it comfortable year-round using minimal energy

plankton—microscopic plants and animals found in saltwater and freshwater that are food for other marine creatures

rain gardens—plantings in shallow depressions designed to collect rainwater from roofs, driveways and other hard surfaces and allow it to soak into the ground rather than cause flooding

renewable resource—a natural resource that is unlimited, such as sunlight or wind, or can be naturally replaced at a rate that is equal to or faster than the rate at which it is consumed

safety bicycle—a type of bicycle that has two wheels of the same size and pedals that turn the back wheel using a chain. They were designed to be much more safe than the high-wheeler (or penny-farthing) bicycle.

sewage—the mixture of liquid and solid wastes that flows down from toilets and drains

sewer system—an underground network of pipes and tunnels that transports sewage away from houses and other buildings

Silk Road—a 4,000-mile (6,400-kilometer) network of trade routes that connected East Asia with Europe. Traders traveled in caravans with camels and other pack animals. Items traded included silk, jade, tea and spices from the East, and glassware, textiles and even horses from the West.

street food—ready-to-eat foods or drinks sold by vendors in the streets or other public places

suburbs—the residential areas on the outskirts of a city or town

tectonic plates—huge slabs of rock that together make up the outer crust of the earth. Tectonic plates are in constant motion, and their movement away from, toward or against each other is what creates mountains, earthquakes and volcanoes.

traffic engineer—a person who helps ensure that city roads are designed safely and that drivers are provided with the information and signs they need to drive safely

typhoid—a bacterial disease, characterized by fever, diarrhea and vomiting, that can be deadly and is often the result of drinking contaminated water

urban heat island—a city area that is warmer than the outlying rural areas because buildings, roads, parking lots and other surfaces absorb and re-emit heat more than natural areas such as forests do

waste pickers—people who salvage reusable or recyclable materials thrown away by others and sell them to support themselves and their families

wastewater—used water from domestic activities, such as bathing, toilet flushing and dishwashing, or from industrial and agricultural activities

wetlands—natural or human-made areas saturated with water, either year-round or during certain seasons. Marshes, bogs and swamps are typical wetlands.

zero waste—a set of principles focused on waste prevention to help eliminate garbage and use fewer resources. The goal is for no trash to be sent to landfills, incinerators or the ocean.

zoning bylaws—regulations that specify how certain areas of land in a city can be used. For example, land can be zoned for houses, for businesses, for industries or for a mix of different uses.

Resources

Print

Briggs Martin, Jacqueline. *Farmer Will Allen and the Growing Table*. Readers to Eaters, 2013.

Clark, Stacy. *Planet Power: Explore the World's Renewable Energy*. Barefoot Books, 2021.

Clendenan, Megan. *Fresh Air, Clean Water: Our Right to a Healthy Environment*. Orca Book Publishers, 2022.

Clendenan, Megan, and Kim Ryall Woolcock. *Design Like Nature: Biomimicry for a Healthy Planet*. Orca Book Publishers, 2021.

Craigie, Gregor. *Why Humans Build Up: The Rise of Towers, Temples and Skyscrapers*. Orca Book Publishers, 2022.

Curtis, Andrea. *City of Water*. Groundwood Books, 2021.

Eamer, Claire. *What a Waste: Where Does Garbage Go?* Annick Press, 2017.

Guillain, Charlotte. *The Street Beneath My Feet*. Words and Pictures by Quarto, 2017.

Jones, Kari. *Ours to Share: Coexisting in a Crowded World*. Orca Book Publishers, 2019.

Mulder, Michelle. *Going Wild: Helping Nature Thrive in Cities*. Orca Book Publishers, 2018.

———. *Home Sweet Neighborhood: Transforming Cities One Block at a Time*. Orca Book Publishers, 2019.

Paeff, Colleen. *The Great Stink: How Joseph Bazalgette Solved London's Poop Pollution Problem*. Margaret K. McElderry Books, 2021.

Peterson, Lois. *Shelter: Homelessness in Our Community*. Orca Book Publishers, 2021.

Online

Child Friendly Cities Initiative: childfriendlycities.org

Earth Observatory's "Cities at Night": earthobservatory.nasa.gov/features/CitiesAtNight

Kids Recycle: kidsrecycle.org

Living Streets: livingstreets.org.uk

Mara Mintzer: How Kids Can Help Design Cities: ted.com/talks/mara_mintzer_how_kids_can_help_design_cities

New York Transit Museum: nytransitmuseum.org

Plant a Seed and See What Grows Foundation: seewhatgrows.org/get-kids-excited-gardening

Acknowledgments

Just like a city, creating a book takes a lot of different departments and a whole lot of cooperation. I'm grateful to urban-planning and history experts Brian Doucet at the University of Waterloo, Patricia Burke Wood at York University, Nicolas Kenny at Simon Fraser University and Jean-Paul David Addie at Georgia State University, who each read parts of the manuscript, pointed out confusing and misleading passages, and generally made the book stronger. Thank you! Any mistakes in the text are mine.

Thank you to all at Orca Book Publishers for producing such amazing books! I'm super grateful to work with everyone in the pod, including my editor, Kirstie Hudson, copyeditor Vivian Sinclair, as well as everyone who worked to make this book beautiful, including Dahlia Yuen, Rachel Page and Georgia Bradburne. I'm so grateful for Suharu Ogawa's amazingly fun illustrations that brought life to the cities. Thank you also to Ruth Linka and Andrew Wooldridge for the opportunity to create this book.

Thanks to my family, Dave and Owen, who patiently listened to me talk incessantly about topics like sewage and solar-powered garbage cans for months.

And a final thanks to all my fabulous neighbors, who kept me supported and sane with fun bike rides, socially distant chats and spontaneous garden visits while I worked on this book during the pandemic. I'm grateful to you all.

Index

*Page numbers in **bold** indicate an image caption.*

Megan Clendenan has lived in all sizes of cities and loves to explore new neighborhoods on foot. She has traveled to school or work by subway, train, bus, bicycle and even by boat. She is the author of *Fresh Air, Clean Water: Our Right to a Healthy Environment* and co-author of *Design Like Nature*, part of the Orca Footprints series. Megan lives near Vancouver, British Columbia, with her family, where she is learning to grow vegetables in her backyard.

Suharu Ogawa is a Toronto-based illustrator. Formally trained in art history and cultural anthropology, she worked for several years as a university librarian until her passion for illustration called her out of that career and into the pursuit of a lifelong dream. Since then Suharu has created illustrations for magazines, public art projects and children's books. She also teaches illustration at OCAD University in Toronto.

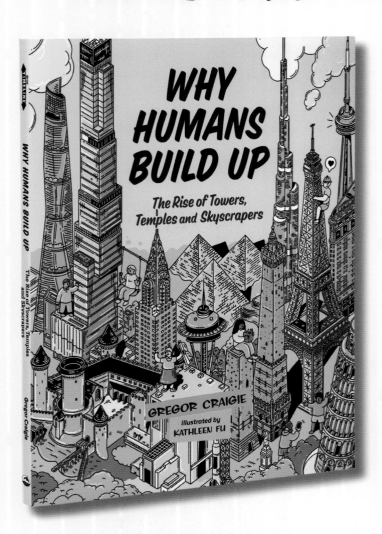

IT'S ABOUT TIME!

Orca TIMELINE

WHY HUMANS BUILD UP
The Rise of Towers, Temples and Skyscrapers

GREGOR CRAIGIE

Illustrated by
KATHLEEN FU

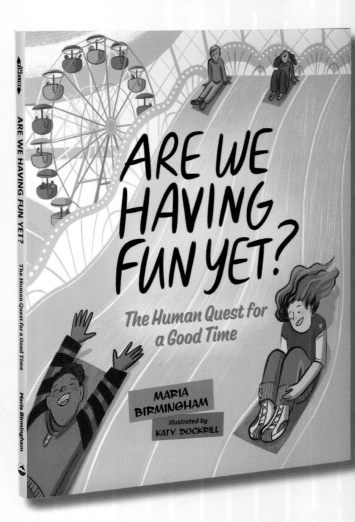

ARE WE HAVING FUN YET?
The Human Quest for a Good Time

MARIA BIRMINGHAM

Illustrated by
KATY DOCKRILL

From the past to the present and into the future, the Orca Timeline series explores how big ideas have shaped humanity. Discover what our collective history can tell us about the planet today and tomorrow.

UPCOMING TOPICS:

Vaccines

Navigation and Transportation

Walls

ORCA